BLOCK *Beauty* QUILTS

Donna Poster

American Quilter's Society

P. O. Box 3290 • Paducah, KY 42002-3290

www.AmericanQuilter.com

Located in Paducah, Kentucky, the American Quilter's Society (AQS) is dedicated to promoting the accomplishments of today's quilters. Through its publications and events, AQS strives to honor today's quiltmakers and their work and to inspire future creativity and innovation in quiltmaking.

Text © 2009, Author, Donna Poster
Artwork © 2009, American Quilter's Society

Executive Book Editor: Andi Milam Reynolds
Graphic Design: Barry Buchanan
Cover Design: Michael Buckingham
Photography: Charles R. Lynch
Additional Editing: Chrystal Abhalter and Linda Baxter Lasco

Additional copies of this book may be ordered from the American Quilter's Society, PO Box 3290, Paducah, KY 42002-3290, or online at www.AmericanQuilter.com.

Library of Congress Cataloging-in-Publication Data

Poster, Donna.
    Block beauty quilts / by Donna Poster.
        p. cm.
    ISBN 978-1-57432-993-3
    1. Patchwork--Patterns. 2. Quilting--Patterns. I. Title.
    TT835.P658 2009
    746.46'041--dc22
                                    2009021357

Contents

Dedication

I dedicate this book to all quilters every-where who find peace and enjoyment from creating something beautiful with fabric.

Introduction

Grandma made gorgeous quilts. Each one was very different from all the others yet she used only two pattern pieces, over and over and over again, to make them all! She loved those two pieces. They were easy to cut, they fit together with no trouble at all, the stitching was easy, and there were endless ways to rearrange them.

In this book I've given you the five quilt patterns I find myself making again and again, plus four very different versions of each — and space for you to doodle on and come up with your own versions! That's what this book is all about. The five patterns are:

RAIL FENCE – An old favorite and great for a beginner to learn basic quilting. Rotary cutting makes it even quicker and easier. Make it for anyone by changing colors – babies, girls, boys, men, the mailman!

X-QUISITE – Looks hard but it's not! After I made MY BATIKS, I learned a neat trick for easy seam matching: it's all in the pressing! Great for scraps but try it in fussy cuts. What fun!

TEXAS TRELLIS – Hard to believe, but there are no "y" or inset seams in this quilt. It's all done in columns. I include a surefire way to match six points. Play with the color placement; the possibilities are endless!

PEAK – It's all done with rectangles! No cutting and piecing little triangles. No guesswork, either. Everybody loves making this pattern, especially if you follow my layout plans.

DRUNKARD'S PATH – If you're scared of curves, this is a good pattern to learn. You'll catch on fast, and you can rotary cut the pieces. Super simple, great results.

How to Use This Book

Each of the five chapters presents the basic instructions for one pattern, and they're presented in order from easiest (Rail Fence) to more challenging (Drunkard's Path). Try the basic pattern for each chapter, and when you've "got it," try making the four variation quilts. Each quilt has its own yardages and instructions for seven different sizes. In addition to alternate color variations, there are blank "doodle" corners for you to try your own combinations.

A few of my own special hints:

• Look over the General Instructions on page 8 before starting.

• Don't rip out seams! Really, unless you've actually put a piece in the wrong place, leave your mismatched seams alone until you're ready to quilt. If you keep ripping out every little mismatched seam as you go along, you'll ruin the fabric and hate the sewing experience. If you enjoy the process, you'll make more quilts and you'll get better and better with the doing.

• So, OK, you're ready to quilt it, but, boy, that seam joining is really bad! Rip about one inch in all directions from the mismatch and ease the pieces till they fit properly (or to your liking). Stitch them back together. Now that wasn't so hard, was it? OK, what's the next worst spot? Does it bother you? If yes, fix it. Keep doing that till you're happy with your quilt top. This little journey helps put things into perspective.

• There are so many possible ways to quilt these "block beauties," I leave it up to you, but I do show you four of the quilting designs used in these quilts.

Color

Choosing colors is one of the most important parts of making a quilt. In my seventeen years of picking out fabrics for customers in my quilt shop, I've come up with a few suggestions:

Start by picking out one fabric that appeals to you and take your color scheme from there. In the end you may not even use that piece of fabric in the top. If not, try using it as the backing. You'll have a lovely reversible quilt.

Look for color schemes that appeal to you. Study quilt magazines, nature, books, etc. I have a stack of ads I've cut out because I like the way the colors work.

Don't over-coordinate. A small accent of an odd color can really make a quilt come to life.

Pay close attention to contrast. A high contrast will set the color scheme of the quilt to the darker of those two fabrics. For example, navy next to white will produce a "navy" quilt, no matter what other colors are in the quilt.

Yellow, if used as an accent, needs to be quite strong.

Solids tend to stand out more than prints. I use a lot of what I call "solid prints"—green on green, blue on blue, etc. They'll give a solid look without the harshness of a solid.

I cut up large prints often to create movement. I then call attention to them by using that fabric in the widest border.

For a dramatic, bold look, use all solids. Magnificent quilts are made with a repetition of one or two blocks using two high-contrast solid fabrics.

Soft prints and low contrast will produce a lovely, subdued, mellow quilt. And, yes, you can use lots of tiny prints together!

Black can add excitement when used to set off brilliant splashes of color. When I made samples for our store, I always seemed to start with a light taupe background, then added color. But darned if I didn't end up (and I mean, always) putting in some black!

Last, don't try to visualize what the quilt will look like in the end. Pick fabrics that work well together, then enjoy watching your quilt come to life!

A Few Words About Scrap Quilts

I confess — scrap quilts are my favorites and all the quilts in this book are great as scrap quilts because they have very few pattern pieces. Complicated designs seldom work well as scrap quilts because the fabrics fight with the design for your attention!

It's easy to get hooked on these quilts because they give you the perfect excuse to buy lots of those gorgeous fat quarters that you just "have to own!" And a scrap quilt can keep a sick child amused for a long time. And they're fun to make! And ... , well, do we really need any more excuses?

There are many ways to approach these quilts. Here are some suggestions:

• To have lots of contrast, keep the lights very light so even the mediums become "darks."

• Don't over-coordinate. The more colors, the better!

• Set up an ongoing scrap quilt. I have a template all set up for the Texas Trellis (page 42). Every time I have scraps from something, I cut out six spokes and add them to the box I've set aside for this project.

• I just can't bring myself to go this far, but a lot of people just throw everything in a bag and use the pieces as they pull them out! And no cheating — what you pull is what you use!

The Basics

• The hardest part about using scraps the first time is getting used to putting an old-fashioned cabbage rose next to a crazy blue dog's butt! Aaagh—but it works!

Remember: There are no rights or wrongs. Try to achieve the look that will make you happy.

Fabric

One hundred percent cotton is the sturdiest choice and has a slight nap, which helps keep the pieces together while stitching.

Buy enough! Fabrics can disappear from the store and never be available again. Extra fabric is great to save for accents, appliqué, scrap quilts, or just to have in your stash.

If you like a fabric, buy it. You may never find it again. If I'm absolutely wild about it, I buy 3 yards. If it's a great background fabric, I'll buy 5 or 6 yards. I'll buy anything I like in a fat quarter just because I "need" to own it!

For my own quilts, I prewash the fabrics for any quilt I think will be laundered someday. I also test for colorfastness by wetting a corner and squeezing it between two sheets of white paper towels. If there is any color bleeding, I wash the fabric again and again till the color is stable. Using a dye fastener such as Retayne also works. I seldom prewash fabrics for wallhangings, as these are not likely to be laundered.

Supplies

The following supplies are quite common in today's quilting scene. Ask for them at your local sewing or quilting store. If you are not close to a store, check online, or visit the vendors during quilt shows.

Rotary-Cutting Equipment - My favorite set is:

• Rotary cutter, bent handle, medium size;

• 18" x 24" cutting mat;

• Ruler for rotary cutting, 24" by at least 6" or more in width;

• 12½" Square Ruler; and

• 60-degree Diamond Shape Ruler for cutting triangles, diamonds, hexagons and wedges.

Fabric - 100% cotton. Buy the best quality you can afford. It's worth it.

¼" Quilter's Tape - A narrow, low residue tape to use on your cutting templates.

Spray Starch - Helps on any fabric that loses its body after laundering.

Long, Large Head Quilting Pins - You won't know how you lived without them!

Safety Pins - Nickel plated, 1" long. About 350 will baste a double bed size quilt.

Sewing Thread - Wind a dozen bobbins with a neutral colored thread and you're set to sew for hours. You may use odds and ends of good quality thread for piecing because it does not have to match the fabric. You will need thread to match the backing fabric (if machine quilting) and to match the binding.

Invisible Thread - For machine quilting.

Quilting Thread - For hand quilting.

Quilting Needles - Hand quilting only. Use "betweens" size 8 to 10. The smaller the needle, the shorter the stitch.

Hand Sewing Needles - For hand sewing use sharps, straws, or milliners, size 10.

Machine Needles - Use a small size (70/10) for piecing. Change it every time you start a new quilt.

Walking Foot or Straight Lines Even-Feed Foot - For machine quilting. It will feed the thicknesses of your quilt evenly.

Darning Foot - For machine quilting. Use for free-motion quilting of designs.

Common Sewing Tools -Scissors, seam ripper, thimble, etc. We all have our favorites.

Thimble - Try them all till you find one you like. It will be worth the effort.

Iron - I prefer a steam iron used gently.

Quilting Stencils - Use to draw quilting lines on a quilt.

Marking Pen (Water Soluble) - Needed to mark quilting lines. If all your quilting follows seamlines, this is not necessary.

Batting - Look for the word "bonded." It holds up well in the washing machine and needs very little quilting.

Lap Frame - For hand quilting small areas at a time.

Hoop or Floor Frame - For hand quilting large quilts.

Bicycle Clips - Using several holds the quilt roll tightly when machine quilting.

Quilt Label - Sign your quilt for security and tell the world you're proud of it!

General Instructions

These basic construction techniques are the ones I've found in my classes to work best for the most people. I feel strongly, however, that quilters must read, listen, experiment, and learn as many hints, techniques, and variations as possible. Gather up a never-ending fund of knowledge, then choose whatever works best for you. If there are ten quilters in the same room, all doing the same thing, they are doing it ten different ways. And they are all correct!

Important! I call the following the "A, B, Cs" of quilting:

A) careful cutting;

B) stitching a perfect, scant ¼ inch seam; and

C) good pressing techniques.

Execute these techniques and your quilting experiences will be much more enjoyable!

Cutting

Most quilt pieces are cut by folding the fabric wrong sides together in the same manner they were folded on the bolt. This produces "mirror-image" pieces (fig. 1).

Fig. 1

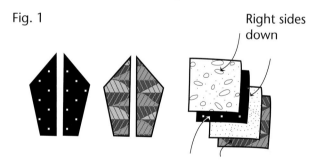

Right sides down

Right sides up

Be careful, though: if "like" image pieces are needed (fig. 2), the pattern will instruct you to stack the fabrics "right-side up." Very important!

Fig. 2

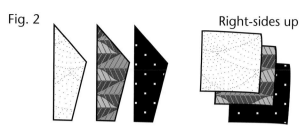

Right-sides up

The first cut will be made to trim the raw edge of the fabric evenly. Position the ruler with the 1" line on the fold of the fabric, ensuring a 90-degree angle and a straight cut when unfolded. Use the ruler as a guide by pressing the cutter gently against the ruler as you cut.

To cut strips, use the strip width to determine the portion of the ruler to place on the fabric (fig. 3). When positioning the ruler, lean over the table and look straight down at it for a straight cut.

Fig. 3

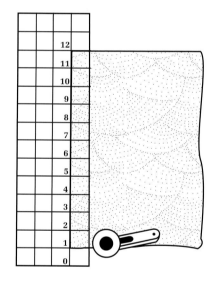

HINT: Put some ¼" masking tape on the ruler line you're using. It's too easy to whiz along and plunk that ruler on the wrong line!

The pattern pieces in this book can be used to cut patches individually or in stacks using a rotary cutter. My preferred method involves taping a ruler with the shape of the template (fig. 4). Use the width of the template piece to cut strips. Use the taped template to cut pieces from those strips (fig. 5).

Fig. 4

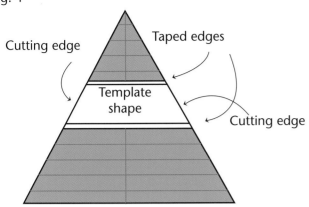

Cutting edge
Taped edges
Template shape
Cutting edge

Fig. 5

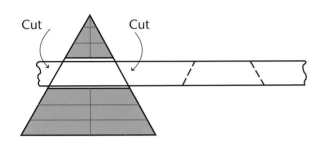

Cut   Cut

To ensure accuracy when cutting small portions from a stack of fabrics, prop the rest of the template on a stack of fabric the same height (fig. 6).

Fig. 6

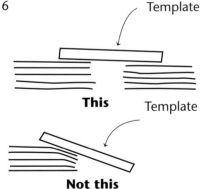

Template

This

Template

Not this

Stitching

You'll find that very little pinning is needed for the patterns in this book. When matching six points and centering curved pieces, a few pins will help, but just nesting the seams together will, with a little practice, produce nicely matched seams (fig. 7). Nest seams

by pressing seam allowances in opposite directions.

Fig. 7

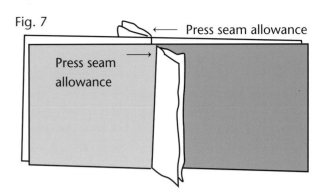

Press seam allowance

Press seam allowance

Why a "scant" ¼ inch seam? There is a bit of loft in the fabric at any seam between the sewn pieces and the seam allowance (fig. 8), creating a shortage in the size of a stitched piece. Sewing the seam just a scant bit smaller (fig. 9) allows for this loft. Test your accuracy by sewing three 2" wide strips together. The unit, after pressing, should measure 5" in width.

Fig. 8

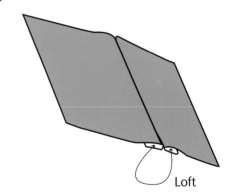

Loft

Fig. 9

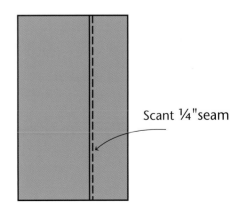

Scant ¼"seam

General Instructions

To establish a ¼" guide, mark a line ¼" away from the edge of a piece of paper. Place the paper under the presser foot and insert the needle into the line. Place tape on your sewing machine surface along the edge of the paper. This will serve as the guide for the cut edge of the fabric as you sew.

Occasionally you'll need to ease two pieces together. Just hold the two ends in place and gently pull the fabric as it is sewn. If possible, sew with the larger piece on the bottom.

> **NOTE**: If sewing bias to bias, never pull to ease. "Pat" them in place instead.

Pressing

Press seams to one side. Whenever possible, press to the darker fabric. Exception: When one seam will be matched to another, press them in opposite directions.

Press with or without steam, as you prefer. Steam can change the shape and size of a piece, though, so use it with caution.

Press from the right side to avoid pleats. Press gently. You are not ironing a pair of blue jeans!

When pressing a piece with a bias edge, gently move the iron with the grain of the bias piece (fig. 10).

Fig. 10

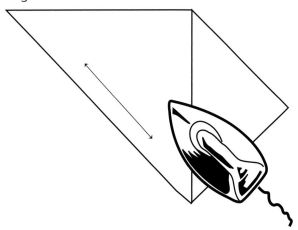

Borders

To add the first border, lay the entire pieced top on a flat surface. Measure down the center of the length of the top. If the top is large, measure at several places and use an average. Cut two border strips to this length.

Pin one border strip to each side edge, right sides together, easing to fit if necessary (fig. 11). Press the seam toward the border. Attach the end borders in the same way (fig. 12).

Fig. 11

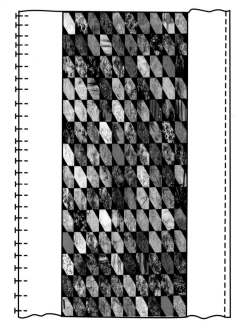

Fig. 12

Add any remaining borders in the same order (sides first, ends last) as the first border, measuring and pinning for accuracy and a flat quilt.

Quilting

To baste the layers together, you'll need a large flat surface such as the floor or a large table. If needed, community centers or church meeting rooms are often available. To ensure a smooth back, tape the backing wrong-side up to the surface. If the quilt is too large for the table, clamp the edges with binder clips to hold it in place. Center the batting on top of the backing. Center the quilt top right-side up on the batting. If machine quilting, use safety pins to pin every 4 to 5 inches apart (fig. 13). If hand quilting, you may prefer to baste with thread. Baste from the center out to the edges so that any fullness or wrinkles will be eased out.

To machine quilt, roll the quilt tightly and fasten with bicycle clips or large pins to manage it under the machine (figs. 14 – 15). The quilt should feed through the machine easily. Be careful not to let the weight of it create a drag.

Check the label on the batting to see how closely it must be quilted. Many batts need very little quilting to be durable. You'll need a walking foot or an even feed foot to control the thickness of the layered quilt. If you are stitching over different colored fabrics, use invisible thread on top. The bobbin should contain thread that matches the quilt backing. Test the stitching. If you use invisible thread you will probably need to lower the tension.

Use a long stitch (6 to 8 per inch). It will feed through easier and give a puffy look. Begin and end with ½" of tightly spaced stitches. As an extra precaution, put quilter's straight pins about every 4 to 6 inches across the quilting line. This will alert you to the quilt being pushed out of shape.

Fig. 13

Fig. 14

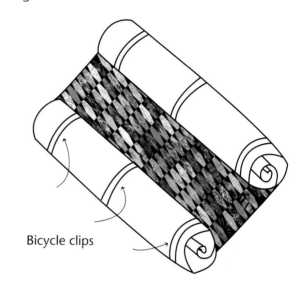

Bicycle clips

Fig. 15

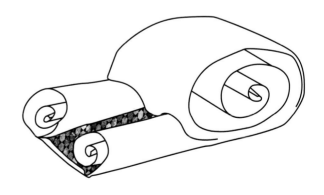

Binding

Cut bias strips 2¼" wide. With right sides together, sew the strips end to end using a ¼" seam (fig 16).

Fig. 16

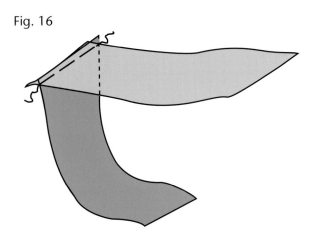

Press the seams open. Fold the joined strip in half lengthwise, wrong sides together (fig. 17). Press.

Fig. 17

Pin the strip to the top edge of the quilt leaving a 6" piece of the strip unattached. Using a scant ⅜" seam, stop stitching ⅜" from the corner, backstitch, and cut the threads. Fold the strip up (fig. 18), then down (fig. 19). The fold should be even with the top edge as shown. Begin stitching at the fold with a ⅜" seam allowance. Continue attaching the binding, stopping and starting as above a seam. Trim the batting and backing even with the raw edge of the top.

Fig. 18

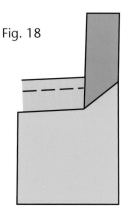

Fig. 19

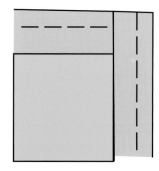

Turn the binding to the back, forming mitered corners. Hand-stitch the folded edge to the quilt back, covering the first line of stitching.

The Rail Fence block is made of three different colored strips sewn together and then cut into blocks. These blocks are then sewn into rows but can be turned this way and that. Fast, fun, easy and flexible! The pattern designs using Rail Fence blocks in this book are: LIGHTNING, PLAID, BASKETWEAVE, and MEDALLION.

Each Rail Fence quilt design will use this block in different arrangements and will have some cutting or sewing variations, but all have these steps in common:

Step 1: Cut all strips 2" wide by the width of your fabric or as specified by the pattern (assume 40" useable). Cut the required number of pieces from each strip or strip-set.

Number of strips in	1/4 yard	1/2 yard	1 yard
2" strips	4	9	18
5" strips	1	3	7

If the design calls for 5" lengths you can get 8 pieces from a 40" strip. If the design calls for 3½" lengths you can get 11 pieces from a 40" strip.

Step 2: Sew three strips together according to the design of your choice (LIGHTNING, PLAID, BASKETWEAVE, MEDALLION) to form a basic strip-set. Press all seams to the darkest fabric. To keep strips from curving, sew each strip in the opposite direction from the previous one, as shown by the arrows.

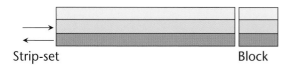

Strip-set   Block

Step 3: Cut blocks from the strip-sets as shown, according to pattern measurements.

NOTE: Although the width of the sewn 2" strip-sets should be 5", if your ¼" seam isn't perfect, this measurement may vary. To achieve blocks whose seams will match and make a straight quilt, measure the width of the strip-set at several places. If the measurements differ, use an average to cut the squares. For example, If your strip-set averages 4¾", cut your squares 4¾" wide. *Caution! The rest of your strip-sets will also have to be 4¾" to yield 4¾" squares.*

Step 4: Sew the blocks together in the design of your choice to form rows. Press seams to the unpieced sections. Sew rows together. Match seams where necessary.

HINT: It's only necessary to match seams where two dark rails meet. This allows a bit of leeway in matching the remaining seams. Press these seams in one direction.

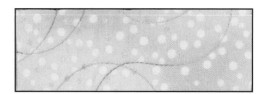

LIGHTNING - 61" x 70"

Pieced by Beth H. Reese, Harrisburg, PA, and Pearl C. Hemphill, Holly Hill, FL
Quilted by Debbie LaDuke, Hummelstown, PA

YARDAGE - LIGHTNING PROJECTS	CRIB	TWIN	DBL	QUEEN	KING	LAP	WALL
Fabric 1 (Lightest)	³/₄	2	2¹/₂	2⁵/₈	3	1¹/₈	³/₈
Fabrics 2, 3, 4 & 5 (each)	³/₈	1¹/₈	1¹/₄	1³/₈	1⁵/₈	⁵/₈	¹/₄
Border 1 (Inner)	¹/₂	⁵/₈	³/₄	³/₄	³/₄	¹/₂	³/₈
Border 2 (Middle)	³/₄	1⁷/₈	1⁷/₈	1	1¹/₈	1¹/₈	¹/₂
Border 3 (Outer) 1*	0	0	0	1¹/₂	1⁵/₈	0	0
Backing	2¹/₂	6¹/₂	8	8¹/₄	10	3³/₄	1¹/₈
Binding	¹/₂	³/₄	⁷/₈	1	1	⁵/₈	¹/₂

* Not shown

LIGHTNING

See page 13 for basic construction of the Rail Fence block and page 14 for yardage.

Step 1: Cut 2" wide strips from all fabrics.

Fabrics:

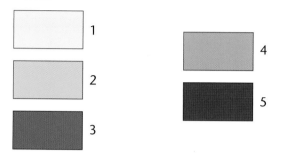

Step 4: Sew the blocks together in rows 1 – 4 as shown, then repeat the pattern of rows. Press block seams to the unpieced sections.

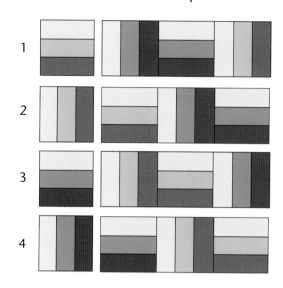

NUMBER OF STRIPS NEEDED

PROJECTS	CRIB	TWIN	DBL	QUEEN	KING	LAP	WALL
Fabric 1 (Lightest)	10	34	40	44	50	18	6
Fabrics 2, 3, 4 & 5 each	5	17	20	22	25	9	3

Step 2: Stitch strips into strip-sets as shown and press the seams to the the darkest fabric.

5"

Strip-set — Block A

Strip-set — Block B

Step 5: Sew the rows together following the block assembly plan on page 16. Match seams where necessary. Press the row seams in the same direction.

Step 6: Add borders as shown on page 10.

CUT BORDER AND BINDING WIDTHS (INCHES)

PROJECTS	CRIB	TWIN	DBL	QUEEN	KING	LAP	WALL
Border 1	2	2	2	2	2	2	2
Border 2	4	6	$5\frac{1}{2}$	3	3	5	4
Border 3	0	0	0	$4\frac{1}{2}$	$4\frac{1}{2}$	0	0
Binding	$2\frac{1}{4}$	$2\frac{1}{4}$	$2\frac{1}{4}$	$2\frac{1}{4}$	$2\frac{1}{4}$	$2\frac{1}{4}$	$2\frac{1}{4}$

Step 3: Cut 5" blocks from these strip-sets. You may have an extra block, depending on the quilt size.

NUMBER OF BLOCKS NEEDED

PROJECTS	CRIB	TWIN	DBL	QUEEN	KING	LAP	WALL
Blocks A & B each	39	130	160	170	200	72	18
BLOCKS IN DESIGN							
Blocks Across	7	13	16	17	20	11	6
Blocks Down	11	20	20	20	20	13	6
Total Blocks	77	260	320	340	400	143	36

Step 7: Quilt, bind, and enjoy!

Block Beauty ■ Donna Poster

Rail Fence: Lightning

LIGHTNING DESIGN AND BLOCK ASSEMBLY PLAN BY QUILT SIZE

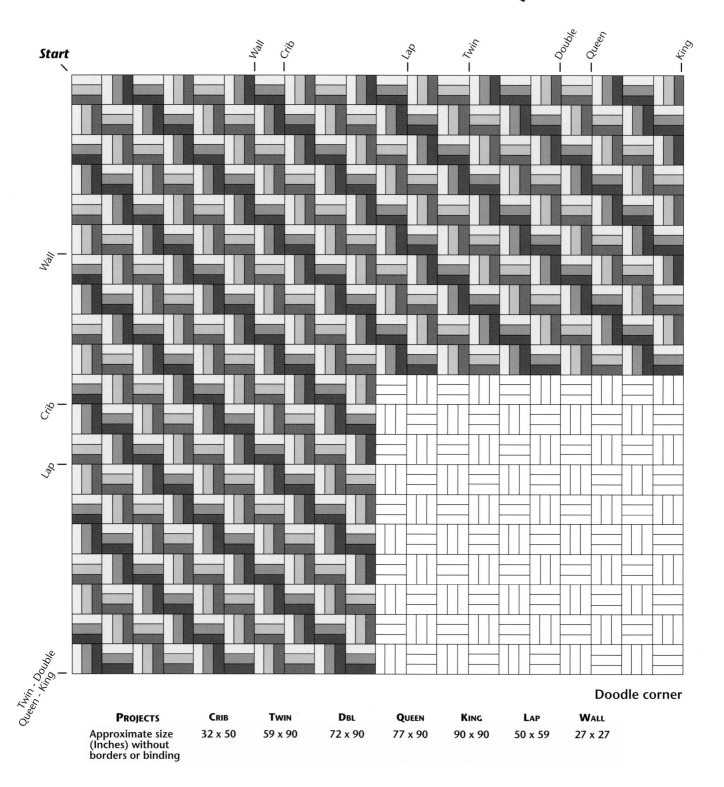

Doodle corner

PROJECTS	CRIB	TWIN	DBL	QUEEN	KING	LAP	WALL
Approximate size (Inches) without borders or binding	32 x 50	59 x 90	72 x 90	77 x 90	90 x 90	50 x 59	27 x 27

PLAID - 52" x 70"

Pieced by Kathy Chickey, Grantville, PA
Quilted by Debbie LaDuke, Hummelstown, PA

YARDAGE - PLAID PROJECTS	CRIB	TWIN	DBL	QUEEN	KING	LAP	WALL
Fabric 1-Block A (Floral)	1/4	7/8	1 1/8	7/8	1	1/2	1/4
Fabric 2-Block B (Medium)	1/4	7/8	1 1/8	5/8	7/8	1/2	1/4
Fabric 3-Block C (Light)	1/2	1 5/8	1 5/8	1 5/8	2	7/8	1/4
Fabrics 4, 5 & 6-Block D (Rails)	3/8	1 1/2	1 1/2	1 1/4	1 1/2	5/8	1/4
Border 1 (Inner)	1/2	5/8	3/4	3/4	3/4	1/2	3/8
Border 2 (Middle)	3/4	1 1/8	1 1/2	1 3/8	1 1/4	1 1/8	1/2
Border 3 (Outer)*	0	0	0	2 1/8	2 1/8	0	0
Backing	2 1/2	6 1/4	8 1/4	8 1/2	9 1/2	3 3/4	1 1/8
Binding	1/2	3/4	7/8	1	1	5/8	1/2

* Not shown

Block Beauty ■ Donna Poster

Rail Fence: Plaid

PLAID

See page 13 for basic construction of the Rail Fence block and yardage chart below.

Step 1: Cut 5" wide strips from fabrics 1, 2 & 3. Cut 2" wide strips from fabrics 4, 5 & 6.

Fabrics:

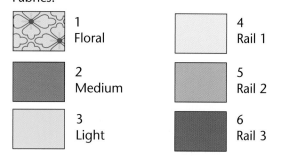

1 Floral	4 Rail 1
2 Medium	5 Rail 2
3 Light	6 Rail 3

NUMBER OF STRIPS NEEDED

PROJECTS	CRIB	TWIN	DBL	QUEEN	KING	LAP	WALL
Fabric 1 (Floral)	1	5	7	4	6	3	1
Fabric 2 (Medium)	1	5	7	4	5	3	1
Fabric 3 (Light)	3	10	10	10	13	5	1
Fabrics 4, 5 & 6 (each)	5	20	23	18	23	9	2

Step 2: Cut 5" blocks from the 5" wide strips.

5"

Block C

Step 3: Stitch the 2" wide strips into strip-sets as shown. These strip-sets should measure 5" wide. Press to the darker of the outer strips. Cut 5" blocks from the strip-sets.

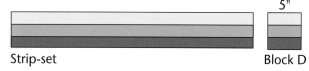

5"

Strip-set   Block D

Blocks A – D are shown below.

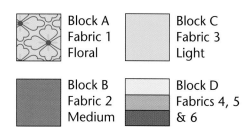

Block A Fabric 1 Floral	Block C Fabric 3 Light
Block B Fabric 2 Medium	Block D Fabrics 4, 5 & 6

NUMBER OF BLOCKS NEEDED

PROJECTS	CRIB	TWIN	DBL	QUEEN	KING	LAP	WALL
BLOCKS OF EACH TYPE							
Blocks A (Floral)	7	39	49	31	41	17	5
Blocks B (Medium)	8	38	50	32	40	18	4
Blocks C (Light)	24	80	80	80	100	36	4
Blocks D (Pieced)	38	158	178	142	180	72	12
BLOCKS IN DESIGN							
Blocks Across	7	15	17	15	19	11	5
Blocks Down	11	21	21	19	19	13	5
Total Blocks	77	315	357	285	361	143	25

Step 4: Sew the blocks together into rows as shown, starting with the center floral A block and repeating the block patterns across according to the number of blocks in your design choice. Refer to the block assembly on page 19. Press the block seams to the unpieced blocks.

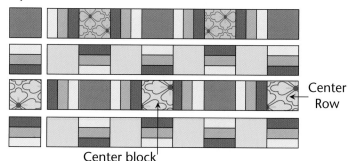

Center Row

Center block

Step 5: Sew rows together starting with the center row, adding rows according to your design choice. Press the row seams toward the rows with the light C blocks.

Step 6: Add borders as shown on page 10.

CUT BORDER AND BINDING WIDTHS (INCHES)

PROJECTS	CRIB	TWIN	DBL	QUEEN	KING	LAP	WALL
Border 1	2	2	2	2	2	2	2
Border 2	4	$3^1/_2$	$4^1/_2$	4	$3^1/_2$	5	4
Border 3	0	0	0	$6^1/_2$	6	0	0
Binding	$2^1/_4$	$2^1/_4$	$2^1/_4$	$2^1/_4$	$2^1/_4$	$2^1/_4$	$2^1/_4$

Step 7: Quilt, bind, and enjoy!

PLAID DESIGN AND BLOCK ASSEMBLY PLAN BY QUILT SIZE

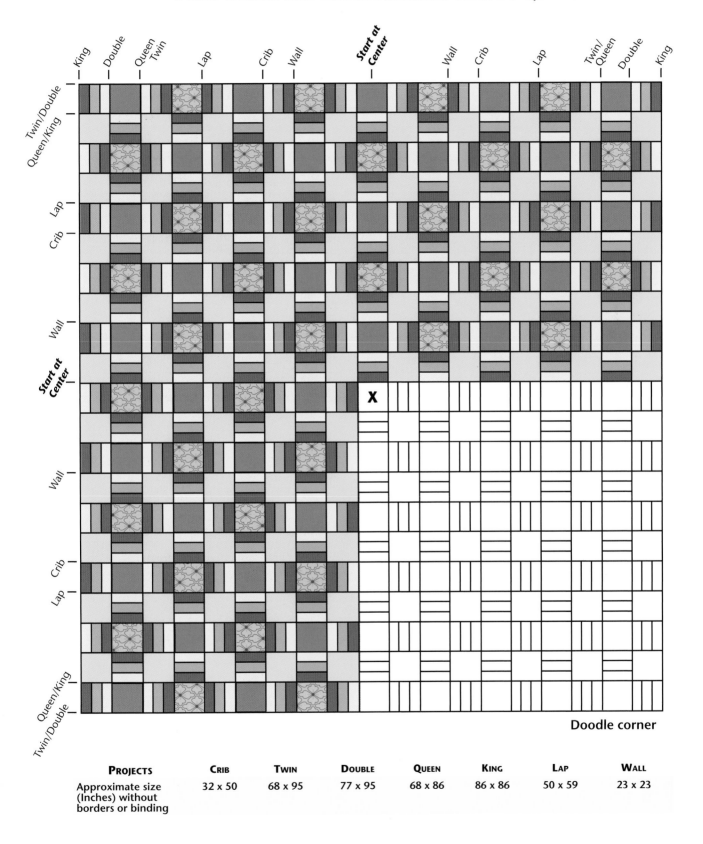

Doodle corner

PROJECTS	CRIB	TWIN	DOUBLE	QUEEN	KING	LAP	WALL
Approximate size (Inches) without borders or binding	32 x 50	68 x 95	77 x 95	68 x 86	86 x 86	50 x 59	23 x 23

Block Beauty ■ Donna Poster

BASKETWEAVE - 60" x 70"

Pieced by Susan DiClemente, Hummelstown, PA
Quilted by Laurel Cook, Mechanicsburg, PA

YARDAGE - BASKETWEAVE PROJECTS	CRIB	TWIN	DBL	QUEEN	KING	LAP	WALL
Fabrics 1 & 2 -- Cross Bars	3/8	1 1/8	1 1/4	1 3/8	1 1/2	5/8	1/4
Fabrics 3, 4 & 5 -- Vertical Strips	1/2	1 1/2	1 3/4	1 7/8	2	7/8	1/4
Border 1 (Inner)	1/2	5/8	3/4	3/4	3/4	1/2	3/8
Border 2 (Middle)	3/4	1 7/8	2 1/8	1	1 1/2	1 1/8	1/2
Border 3 (Outer)*	0	0	0	1 1/2	2	0	0
Backing	2 1/2	6 1/2	8 1/4	8 1/4	10	4	1 1/8
Binding	1/2	3/4	7/8	1	1	5/8	1/2

* Not shown

BASKETWEAVE

See page 13 for basic construction of the Rail Fence block and page 20 for yardage.

Step 1: Cut 2" wide strips from all fabrics.

Fabrics:

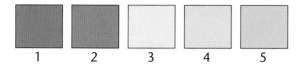

1 2 3 4 5

NUMBER OF STRIPS NEEDED

PROJECTS	CRIB	TWIN	DBL	QUEEN	KING	LAP	WALL
Fabric 1 (Cross Rail 1)	6	18	20	23	24	10	2
Fabric 2 (Cross Rail 2)	5	15	18	20	22	9	2
Fabrics 3, 4 & 5 (Each) Vertical Rails	7	24	28	31	33	13	3

Step 2: Cut 5" lengths from fabrics 1 and 2.

1

2

5"

Sew strips of fabrics 3, 4 and 5 into strip-sets as shown. Press to the darkest outer strip.

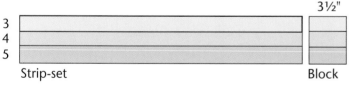

3
4
5

Strip-set

Block

3½"

Step 3: Cut 3½" segments from the strip-sets to form strip blocks.

Step 4: Sew the 5" strips to the strip blocks to form Blocks A & B. Press to the 5" strip.

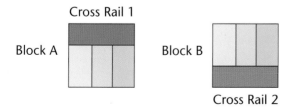

Cross Rail 1

Block A

Block B

Cross Rail 2

NUMBER OF BLOCKS NEEDED

PROJECTS	CRIB	TWIN	DBL	QUEEN	KING	LAP	WALL
BLOCKS OF EACH TYPE							
Block A	44	140	160	180	190	78	15
Block B	33	120	140	160	171	65	10
BLOCKS IN DESIGN							
Blocks Across	7	13	15	17	19	11	5
Blocks Down	11	20	20	20	19	13	5
Total Blocks	77	260	300	340	361	143	25

Step 5: Sew the blocks into columns as shown. Press block seams toward the unpieced part of the blocks.

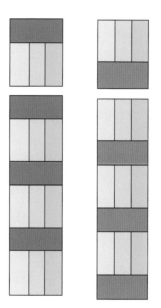

Step 6: Sew the columns together according to the block assembly plan on page 22, starting with Block A at the upper left corner. Press row seams to the columns of A blocks.

Step 7: Add borders as shown on page 10.

CUT BORDER AND BINDING WIDTHS (INCHES)

PROJECTS	CRIB	TWIN	DBL	QUEEN	KING	LAP	WALL
Border 1	2	2	2	2	2	2	2
Border 2	4	6	6½	3	4	5	4
Border 3	0	0	0	4½	5½	0	0
Binding	2¼	2¼	2¼	2¼	2¼	2¼	2¼

Step 8: Quilt, bind, and enjoy!

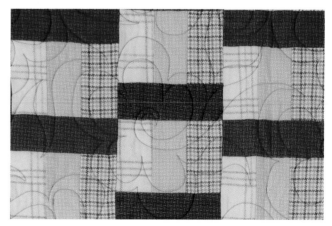

BASKETWEAVE DESIGN AND BLOCK ASSEMBLY PLAN BY QUILT SIZE

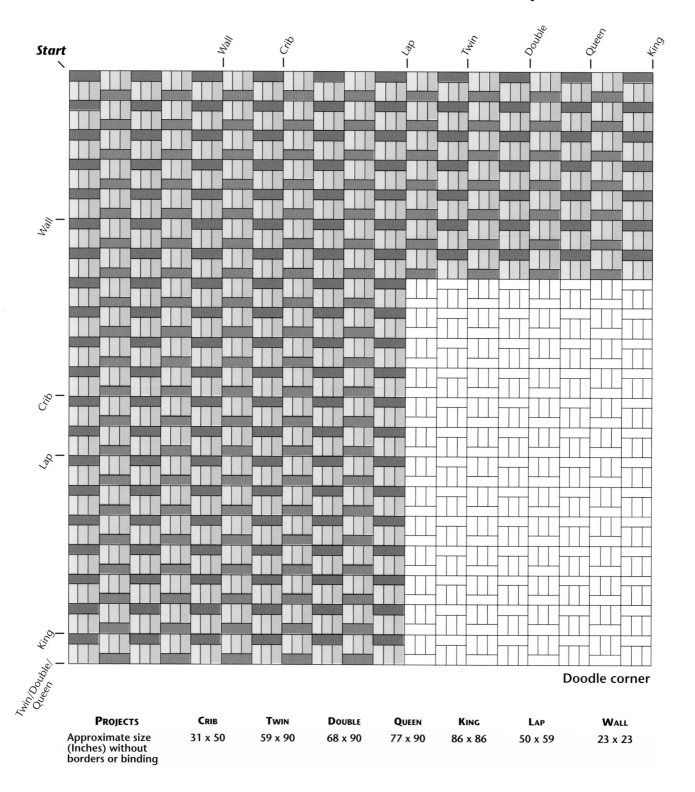

Doodle corner

PROJECTS	CRIB	TWIN	DOUBLE	QUEEN	KING	LAP	WALL
Approximate size (Inches) without borders or binding	31 x 50	59 x 90	68 x 90	77 x 90	86 x 86	50 x 59	23 x 23

MEDALLION - 63" x 72"

Pieced and quilted by Ellen Oliver, Carlisle, PA

YARDAGE - MEDALLION PROJECTS	CRIB	TWIN	DBL	QUEEN	KING	LAP	WALL
Block A: Fabric 1 (Dark) & Fabric 2 (Med) Each	3/8	1 1/8	1 1/4	1 1/4	1 5/8	3/4	1/4
Blocks A & B: Fabric 3 - (Light)	3/4	2 1/8	2 1/2	2 1/2	3	1 3/8	3/8
Block B: Fabric 4 - (Accent) & Fabric 5 (Lightest)	3/8	1 1/8	1 1/4	1 1/4	1 5/8	3/4	1/4
Border 1	1 3/4	5/8	3/4	3/4	3/4	1/2	3/8
Border 2	0	1 1/2	1 5/8	1	1 1/8	7/8	1/2
Border 3*	0	0	0	1 1/2	1 5/8	0	0
Backing	2 3/4	6 1/4	8	8 1/2	10	4	1 1/4
Binding	1/2	3/4	7/8	1	1	5/8	1/2

* Not shown

MEDALLION

See page 13 For basic construction of the Rail Fence block and page 23 for yardage.

Step 1: Cut 2" wide strips from all of the fabrics.

Fabrics:

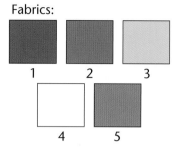

1 2 3

4 5

NUMBER OF STRIPS NEEDED

PROJECTS	CRIB	TWIN	DBL	QUEEN	KING	LAP	WALL
Fabrics 1 & 2 Strips (Each)	6	18	20	20	26	11	3
Fabric 3 Strips (Blocks A & B)	12	35	40	40	51	21	5
Fabrics 4 & 5 Strips (Each)	6	17	20	20	25	10	2

Step 2: Sew strips of fabrics 1, 2 & 3 into strip-sets. Sew strips of fabrics 3, 4 & 5 into strip-sets. Press to the darkest fabric. The strip-sets should measure 5" wide.

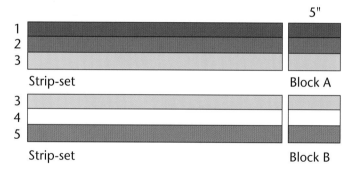

5"

1
2
3

Strip-set   Block A

3
4
5

Strip-set   Block B

Step 3: Cut 5" blocks from these strip-sets for Blocks A and B.

NUMBER OF BLOCKS NEEDED

PROJECTS	CRIB	TWIN	DBL	QUEEN	KING	LAP	WALL
BLOCKS OF EACH TYPE							
Block A	24	72	80	80	102	44	10
Block B	24	68	80	80	98	40	8
BLOCKS IN DESIGN							
Blocks Across	8	14	16	16	20	12	6
Blocks Down	12	20	20	20	20	14	6
Total Blocks	96	280	320	320	400	168	36

Step 4: Sew Blocks A & B to form units A, AA, B, and BB as shown. Press cross (horizontal) seams up on Unit A and down on Unit B.

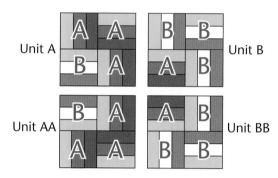

Unit A   Unit B

Unit AA   Unit BB

Step 5: Arrange the units to form the design, starting in the center. Stitch together. Press seams in opposite directions.

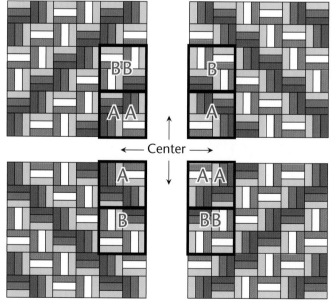

← Center →

Step 6: Arrange the units as shown in the block assembly plan on page 26.

Step 7: Add borders as shown on page 10.

CUT BORDER AND BINDING WIDTHS (INCHES)

PROJECTS	CRIB	TWIN	DBL	QUEEN	KING	LAP	WALL
Border 1	$3^1/_2$	2	2	2	2	2	2
Border 2	0	5	5	3	3	4	4
Border 3	0	0	0	$4^1/_2$	$4^1/_2$	0	0
Binding	$2^1/_4$	$2^1/_4$	$2^1/_4$	$2^1/_4$	$2^1/_4$	$2^1/_4$	$2^1/_4$

Step 8: Quilt, bind, and enjoy!

Rail Fence: Medallion

MEDALLION DESIGN AND BLOCK ASSEMBLY PLAN BY QUILT SIZE

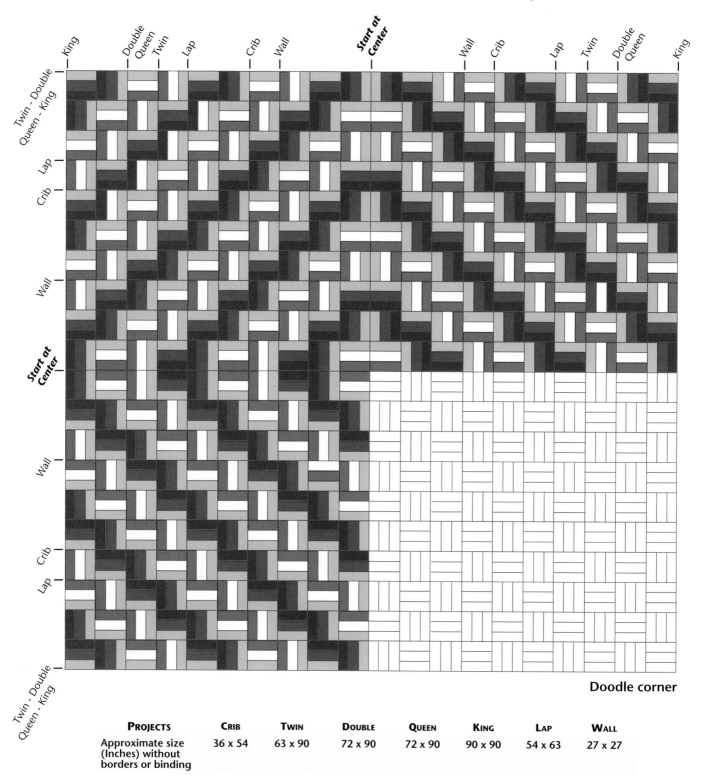

Doodle corner

PROJECTS	CRIB	TWIN	DOUBLE	QUEEN	KING	LAP	WALL
Approximate size (Inches) without borders or binding	36 x 54	63 x 90	72 x 90	72 x 90	90 x 90	54 x 63	27 x 27

X-Quisite: Basic Construction

The 5" X-Quisite block is made of templates A and B on page 28. Sometimes you contrast one B piece with A, sometimes both B pieces. In addition to that variation, whichever way you turn the finished block, you get a different result:

LATTICE

MY BATIKS

STARS

BUTTERFLIES

Each quilt design in this chapter will use this block in different arrangements and will have some cutting or sewing variations, but some techniques apply to them all.

X-Quisite: Basic Construction

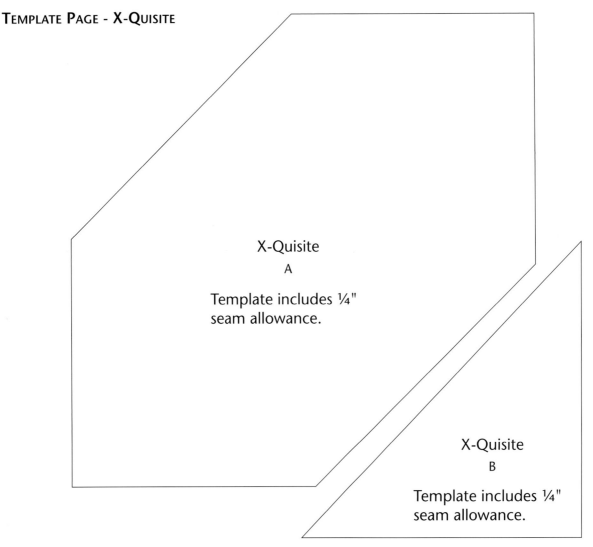

X-Quisite

A

Template includes ¼"
seam allowance.

X-Quisite

B

Template includes ¼"
seam allowance.

Piece A: Cut strips 5" wide. Cut 5" x 5" squares from the strips (8 from each 40" strip).

Cut out an A template and tape it to the underside of a rotary ruler as shown (A).

Align the points of the template with the corners of a fabric square and trim off the corner (B). Turn and repeat to trim off the opposite corner.

Piece B: Cut strips 3¹/₈" wide. Cut 3¹/₈" x 3¹/₈" squares from the strips (12 squares from each 40" strip, making 24 triangles when cut in half).

Cut the squares in half on the diagonal (C).

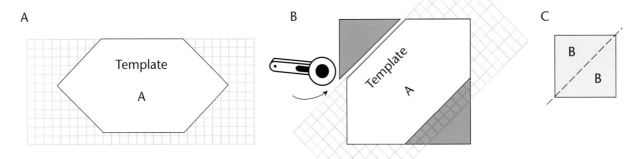

BASIC CONSTRUCTION

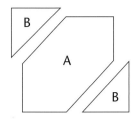

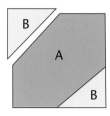

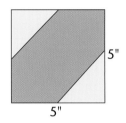

Hint on matching the points: I found it best to have the points just a "skootch" off, as shown below. And, yes, we quilters do know what a skootch is! Try a few and see what works for you.

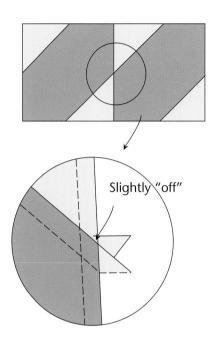

Slightly "off"

Step 1: Sew 2 B pieces to each A piece to make the block.

Step 2: Sew the blocks together in rows according to the quilt design. Press the block seams in opposite directions.

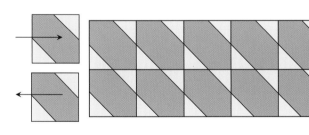

Step 3: Sew the rows together. Press the row seams in the same direction.

Lattice - 55" x 73"

Pieced by the author
Quilted by Debbie LaDuke, Hummelstown, PA

Yardage -Lattice Projects	Crib	Twin	Dbl	Queen	King	Lap	Wall
Fabric 1 - Lattice	$1^3/_4$	5	$5^3/_4$	$6^1/_2$	$7^1/_4$	$2^5/_8$	$^3/_4$
Fabric 2 - Background	$^3/_4$	$2^1/_4$	$2^1/_2$	$2^3/_4$	$3^1/_8$	$1^1/_4$	$^7/_8$
Fabric 3 - Border 1	$^5/_8$	$^5/_8$	$^5/_8$	$^3/_4$	1	$^1/_2$	$^3/_8$
Fabric 4 - Border 2	$1^7/_8$	3	3	$3^1/_8$	$3^1/_8$	$2^1/_8$	$1^1/_8$
Fabric 5 - Backing	$2^1/_2$	6	6	$7^1/_2$	9	$4^1/_2$	$1^1/_8$

LATTICE

See pages 28–29 for basic construction of the X-Quisite block. The yardage chart is on page 30.

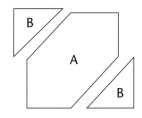

NUMBER OF PIECES NEEDED

PROJECTS	CRIB	TWIN	DBL	QUEEN	KING	LAP	WALL
Fabric 1 A Pieces	96	280	320	360	400	140	36
Fabric 2 B Pieces	192	560	640	720	800	280	72

Number of pieces in	¹/₄ yard	¹/₂ yard	1 yard
Pieces A	8	24	48
Pieces B	48	120	240

Step 1: Sew 2 B pieces to each A piece. Press the seams in one direction as shown.

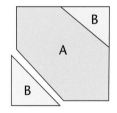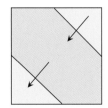

NUMBER OF BLOCKS NEEDED

PROJECTS	CRIB	TWIN	DBLE	QUEEN	KING	LAP	WALL
Blocks Across	8	14	16	18	20	10	6
Blocks Down	12	20	20	20	20	14	6
Total Blocks	96	280	320	360	400	140	36

Step 2: Sew the blocks together in rows. To match points, position the blocks so seams "nestle" into each other. Press the block seams in opposite directions as shown.

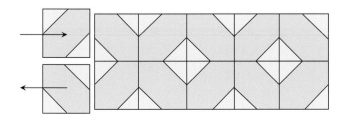

Step 3: Sew the rows together according to the block assembly plan page 32. Press all the row seams in one direction.

CUT BORDER AND BINDING WIDTHS (INCHES)

PROJECTS	CRIB	TWIN	DBL	QUEEN	KING	LAP	WALL
Border 1	3¹/₂	2	2	2¹/₂	2¹/₂	2	2
Border 2	0	5	5¹/₂	6¹/₂	6¹/₂	5	3¹/₂
Binding	2¹/₄	2¹/₄	2¹/₄	2¹/₄	2¹/₄	2¹/₄	2¹/₄

Step 4: Add borders as shown on page 10.

Step 5: Quilt, bind, and enjoy!

X-Quisite: Lattice

LATTICE DESIGN AND BLOCK ASSEMBLY PLAN BY QUILT SIZE

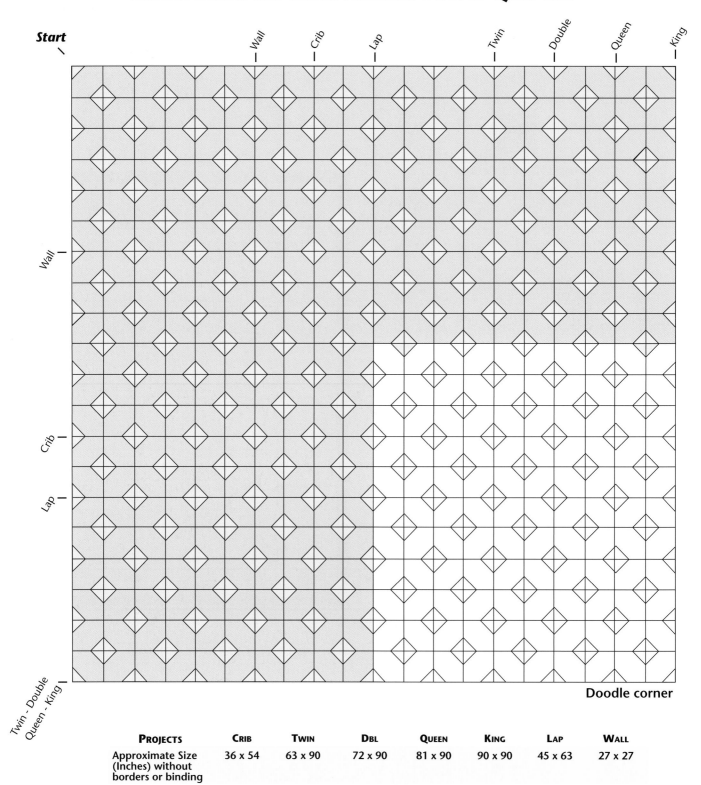

Start

Wall   Crib   Lap   Twin   Double   Queen   King

Wall

Crib

Lap

Twin - Double
Queen - King

Doodle corner

PROJECTS	CRIB	TWIN	DBL	QUEEN	KING	LAP	WALL
Approximate Size (Inches) without borders or binding	36 x 54	63 x 90	72 x 90	81 x 90	90 x 90	45 x 63	27 x 27

MY BATIKS - 55" x 73"

Pieced and quilted by the author

YARDAGE - MY BATIK PROJECTS	CRIB	TWIN	DBL	QUEEN	KING	LAP	WALL
Fabric 1 – Centers*	$1/4$	$5/8$	$5/8$	$3/4$	$3/4$	$3/8$	$1/8$
Fabric 2 – Background	$3/4$	$2^1/4$	$2^1/2$	$2^3/4$	$3^1/8$	$1^1/4$	$7/8$
Border 1	$5/8$	$5/8$	$5/8$	$3/4$	1	$1/2$	$3/8$
Border 2	$1^7/8$	3	3	$3^1/8$	$3^1/8$	$2^1/8$	$1^1/8$
Backing	$2^1/2$	6	6	$7^1/2$	9	$4^1/2$	$1^1/8$

* Each of 10 fabrics

X-Quisite: My Batiks

MY BATIKS

See pages 28–29 for basic construction of the X-Quisite block. The yardage chart is on page 33.

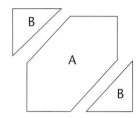

NUMBER OF PIECES NEEDED

PROJECTS	CRIB	TWIN	DBL	QUEEN	KING	LAP	WALL
Fabric 1 A* Pieces	10	28	32	36	40	14	4
Fabric 2 B Pieces	192	560	640	720	800	280	72

* Each of 10 fabrics; you will have a few extra pieces.

Number of pieces in	1/4 yard	1/2 yard	1 yard
A Pieces	8	24	48
B Pieces	48	120	240

Step 1: Sew 2 B pieces to each A piece. Press the seams toward the triangles as shown.

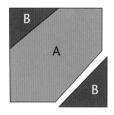 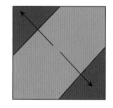

NUMBER OF BLOCKS NEEDED

PROJECTS	CRIB	TWIN	DBL	QUEEN	KING	LAP	WALL
Blocks Across	8	14	16	18	20	10	6
Blocks Down	12	20	20	20	20	14	6
Total Blocks	96	280	320	360	400	140	36

Step 2: Sew the blocks together in rows according to the block assembly plan on page 35. To match points, position the blocks slightly off, as shown in step 2 on page 29. Press the block seams in opposite directions as shown.

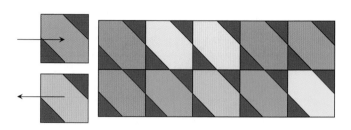

Step 3: Sew the rows together. Press all the row seams in one direction.

Step 4: Add borders as shown on page 10.

CUT BORDER AND BINDING WIDTHS (INCHES)

PROJECTS	CRIB	TWIN	DBL	QUEEN	KING	LAP	WALL
Border 1	3 1/2	2	2	2 1/2	2 1/2	2	2
Border 2	0	5	5 1/2	6 1/2	6 1/2	5	3 1/2
Binding	2 1/4	2 1/4	2 1/4	2 1/4	2 1/4	2 1/4	2 1/4

Step 5: Quilt, bind, and enjoy!

MY BATIKS DESIGN AND BLOCK ASSEMBLY PLAN BY QUILT SIZE

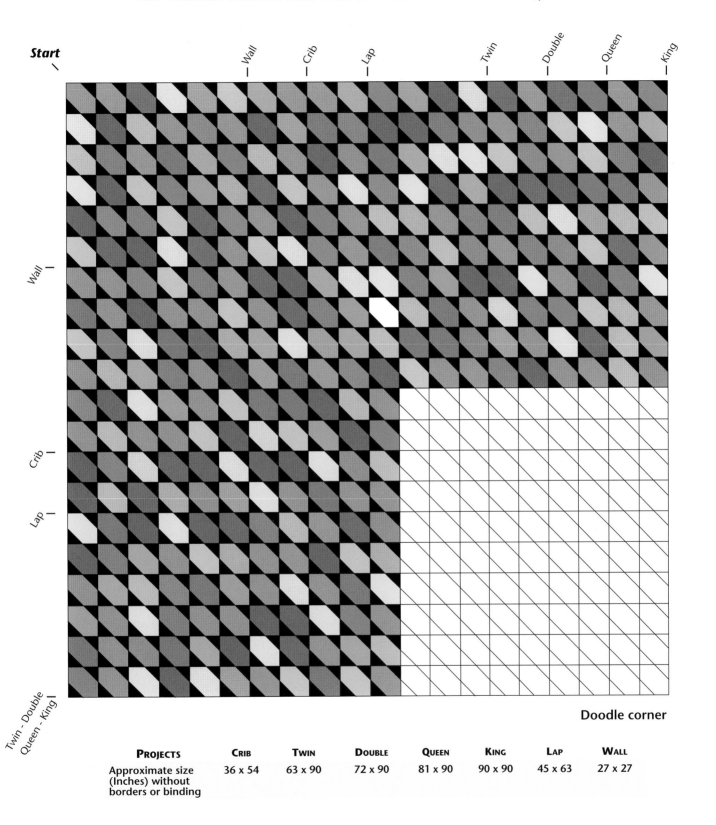

Doodle corner

PROJECTS	CRIB	TWIN	DOUBLE	QUEEN	KING	LAP	WALL
Approximate size (Inches) without borders or binding	36 x 54	63 x 90	72 x 90	81 x 90	90 x 90	45 x 63	27 x 27

Block Beauty ■ Donna Poster

STARS - 55" x 73"

Pieced and quilted by the author

YARDAGE - STARS PROJECTS	CRIB	TWIN	DBL	QUEEN	KING	LAP	WALL
Fabric 1 – Star Points	$3/4$	$2^1/4$	$2^1/2$	$2^3/4$	$3^1/8$	$1^1/4$	$7/8$
Fabric 2 – Star Centers	$5/8$	$1^3/4$	$2^1/8$	$2^1/4$	$2^1/2$	1	$3/8$
Fabric 3 – Background	$1^1/8$	$3^1/2$	4	$4^1/2$	$4^7/8$	$1^3/4$	$1/2$
Border 1	$5/8$	$5/8$	$5/8$	$3/4$	1	$1/2$	$3/8$
Border 2	$1^7/8$	3	3	$3^1/8$	$3^1/8$	$2^1/8$	$1^1/8$
Backing	$2^1/2$	6	6	$7^1/2$	9	$4^1/2$	$1^1/8$

STARS

See pages 28–29 for basic construction of the X-Quisite block. The yardage chart is on page 36.

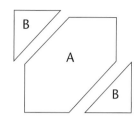

Fabrics:

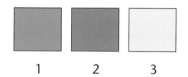

1   2   3

NUMBER OF PIECES NEEDED

PROJECTS	CRIB	TWIN	DBL	QUEEN	KING	LAP	WALL
Fabric 1 - B Pieces	192	560	640	720	800	280	72
Fabric 2 - A Pieces	32	94	107	120	134	47	12
Fabric 3 - A Pieces	64	188	214	240	268	94	24

Number of pieces in	1/4 yard	1/2 yard	1 yard
Piece A	8	24	48
Pieces B	48	120	240

Step 1: Sew 2 B pieces to each A piece. Press the seams toward the triangles as shown.

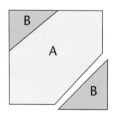 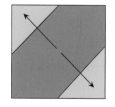

NUMBER OF BLOCKS NEEDED

PROJECTS	CRIB	TWIN	DBL	QUEEN	KING	LAP	WALL
Blocks Across	8	14	16	18	20	10	6
Blocks Down	12	20	20	20	20	14	6
Blocks Blocks	96	280	320	360	400	140	36

Step 2: Sew the blocks together in rows. To match points see step 2 on page 29. Press rows in opposite directions as shown.

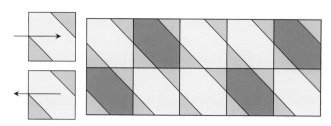

Step 3: Sew the rows together according to the block assembly plan on page 38. Press the row seams in one direction.

Step 4: Add borders as shown on page 10.

CUT BORDER AND BINDING WIDTHS (INCHES)

PROJECTS	CRIB	TWIN	DBL	QUEEN	KING	LAP	WALL
Border 1 (Inches)	3 1/2	2	2	2 1/2	2 1/2	2	2
Border 2 (Inches)	0	5	5 1/2	6 1/2	6 1/2	5	3 1/2
Binding	2 1/4	2 1/4	2 1/4	2 1/4	2 1/4	2 1/4	2 1/4

Step 5: Quilt, bind, and enjoy!

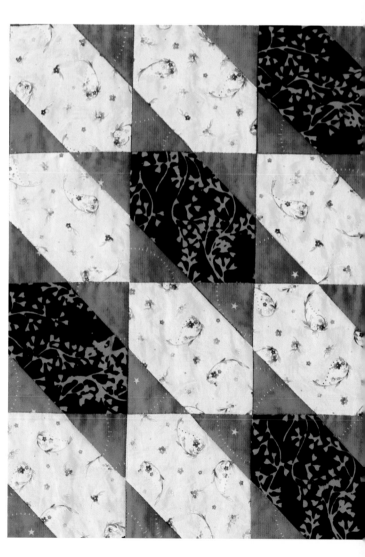

STARS DESIGN AND BLOCK ASSEMBLY PLAN BY QUILT SIZE

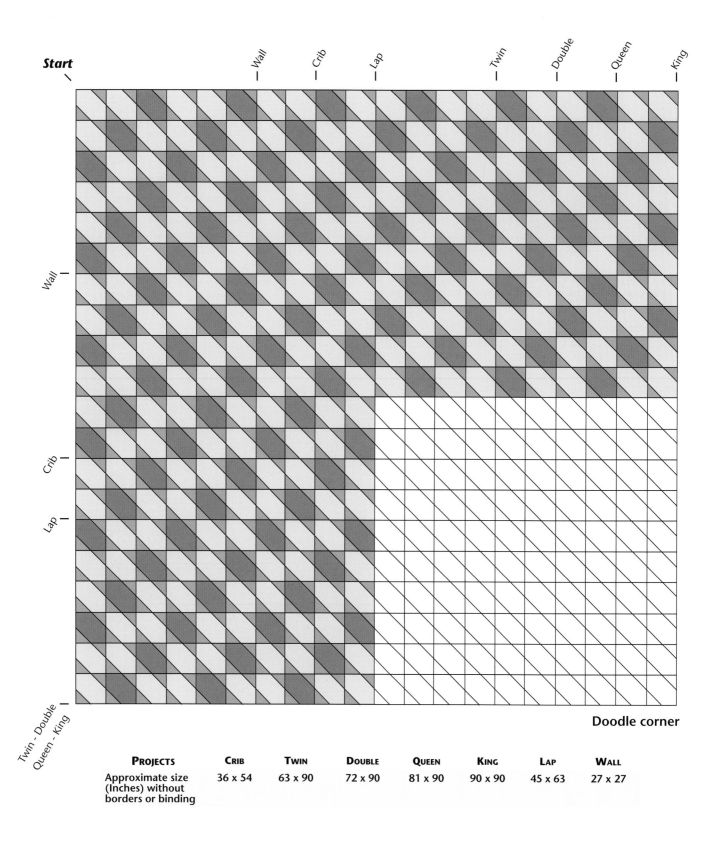

Doodle corner

PROJECTS	CRIB	TWIN	DOUBLE	QUEEN	KING	LAP	WALL
Approximate size (Inches) without borders or binding	36 x 54	63 x 90	72 x 90	81 x 90	90 x 90	45 x 63	27 x 27

BUTTERFLIES - 55" x 73"

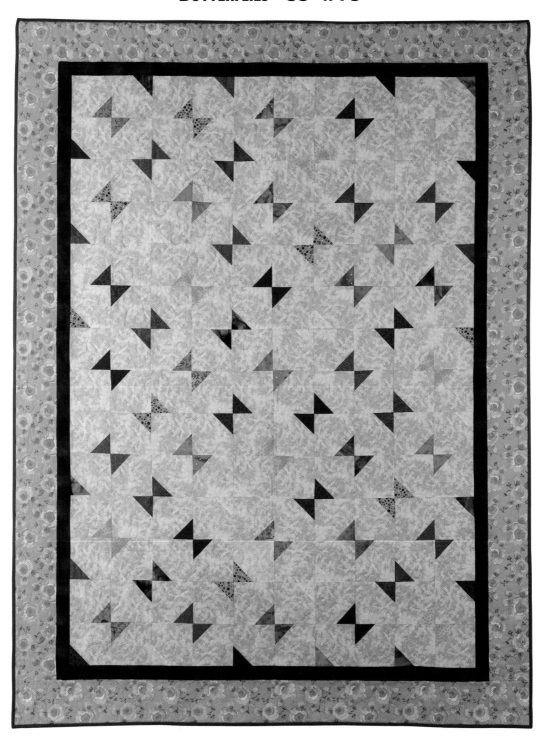

Pieced by the author
Quilted by Debbie LaDuke, Hummelstown, PA

YARDAGE - BUTTERFLIES PROJECTS	CRIB	TWIN	DBL	QUEEN	KING	LAP	WALL
Fabric 1 – Butterflies*	1/4	1 1/8	1 3/8	1 1/2	1 1/2	5/8	1/4
Fabric 2 – Background	1 3/4	5	5 3/4	6 1/2	6 5/8	2 5/8	3/4
Border 1	5/8	5/8	5/8	3/4	1	1/2	3/8
Border 2	1 7/8	3	3	3 1/8	3 1/8	2 1/8	1 1/8
Backing	2 1/2	6	6	7 1/2	9	4 1/2	1 1/8

* Use scraps if you like.

X-Quisite: Butterflies

BUTTERFLIES

CUTTING NOTE - Cut off only one corner on the A piece as shown below.

See pages 28–29 for basic construction of the X-Quisite block. The yardage chart is on page 39.

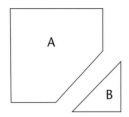

NUMBER OF PIECES NEEDED

PROJECTS	CRIB	TWIN	DBL	QUEEN	KING	LAP	WALL
Fabric 1 - A Pieces	96	280	320	360	400	140	36
Fabric 2 - B Pieces	96	280	320	360	400	140	36

Number of pieces in	1/4 yard	1/2 yard	1 yard
A Pieces	8	24	48
B Pieces	48	120	240

Step 1: Sew the one B piece to each A piece. Press the block seam toward the triangle.

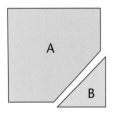 

NUMBER OF BLOCKS NEEDED

PROJECTS	CRIB	TWIN	DBL	QUEEN	KING	LAP	WALL
Blocks Across	8	14	16	18	20	10	6
Blocks Down	12	20	20	20	20	14	6
Total Blocks	96	280	320	360	400	140	36

Step 2: Sew the blocks together in rows. Note the direction of the triangles, giving a sense of flight. Press the block seams in opposite directions.

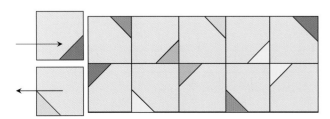

Step 3: Sew the rows together according to the block assembly plan on page 41. Press all the seams in the same direction.

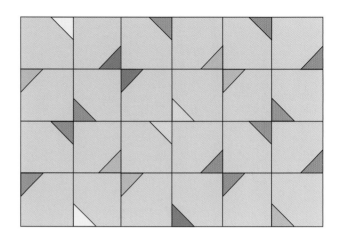

Step 4: Add borders as shown on page 10.

CUT BORDER AND BINDING WIDTHS (INCHES)

PROJECTS	CRIB	TWIN	DBL	QUEEN	KING	LAP	WALL
Border 1	3½	2	2	2½	2½	2	2
Border 2	0	5	5½	6½	6½	5	3½
Binding	2¼	2¼	2¼	2¼	2¼	2¼	2¼

Step 5: Quilt, bind, and enjoy!

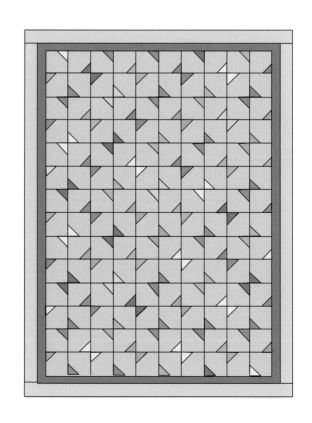

BUTTERFLIES DESIGN AND BLOCK ASSEMBLY PLAN BY QUILT SIZE

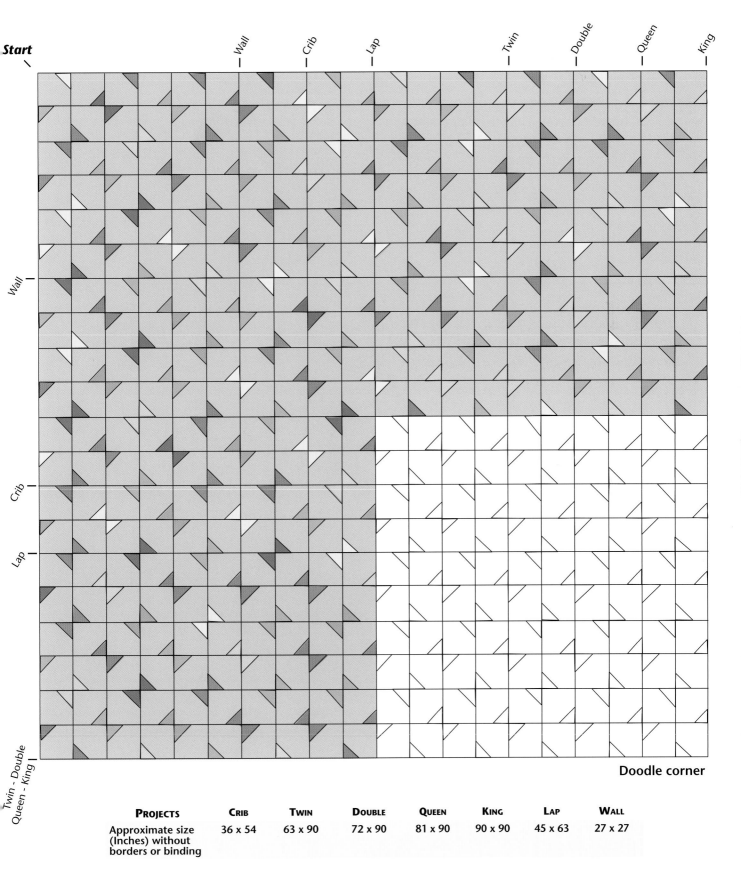

Doodle corner

PROJECTS	CRIB	TWIN	DOUBLE	QUEEN	KING	LAP	WALL
Approximate size (Inches) without borders or binding	36 x 54	63 x 90	72 x 90	81 x 90	90 x 90	45 x 63	27 x 27

41

Texas Trellis: Basic Construction

The Texas Trellis block is made of templates A and B on page 43. 6 units of the rows are completed with end pieces cut from a rectangle (fig.3 on page 43). What looks complicated is easy because you sew the designs together in columns instead of by blocks.

The trick to making any of these designs work is to be very careful as you place and sew each unit. Getting them mixed up is easy — and part of the challenge!

WHIRLIGIG

TAPESTRY

RICKRACK

CONFETTI

Each quilt design in this chapter will use this block in different arrangements and will have some cutting or sewing variations, but some techniques apply to them all.

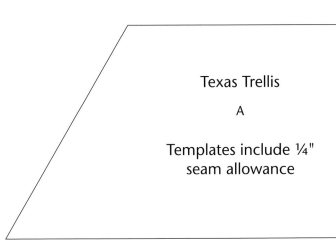

Texas Trellis

A

Templates include ¼"
seam allowance

Piece A: Cut strips 2¹/₄" wide. Cut out an A template and tape it to the underside of a 60-degree rotary ruler, aligning the template edges with the edges of the ruler.

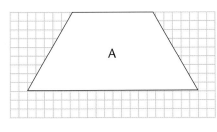

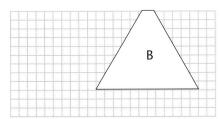

Align the template with the strip and cut A pieces, alternating the placement of the ruler as shown. Each 40" strip will yield 10 A pieces.

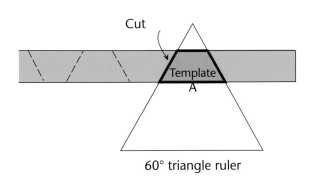

Cut

60° triangle ruler

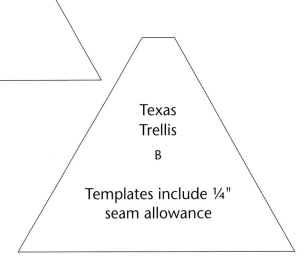

Texas
Trellis

B

Templates include ¼"
seam allowance

Piece B: Repeat these steps using the B template. Each 40" strip will yield 22 B pieces.

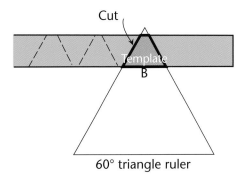

Cut

60° triangle ruler

End Pieces: Stack the fabric with wrong sides together and cut 5" x 3" rectangles. Cut them diagonally as shown. A stack of 2 fabrics makes 4 end pieces.

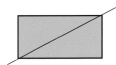

BASIC CONSTRUCTION

> **HINT**: Wedges and triangles have a lot of bias edges. Handle them carefully without stretching. Pin as needed. When stitching a seam, gently "help" it under the presser foot to avoid pulling on the seam.

Step 1: Join the A & B pieces as shown to form triangles. Press the seams toward the A pieces.

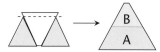

Step 2: Join 3 pieced triangles to make half hexagon units. Sew with the bias edges on the bottom and the long edge of the A piece on top.

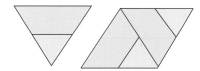

Press seams toward the A pieces as shown to create a half hexagon unit.

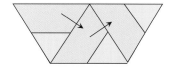

> **HINT**: Look out, it's very easy to sew a few of these units going in the opposite direction from the others! I know, I've done it!

Step 3: Join the half hexagon units in columns, beginning and ending with end pieces. This example happens to be whirligig. The end pieces will be a bit too large. Let the sharper points extend. This allows you to trim later if needed. Press the the seams of odd number columns up, even number columns down.

Col. 1 Col. 2   Col. 1 Col. 2   Col. 1 Col. 2

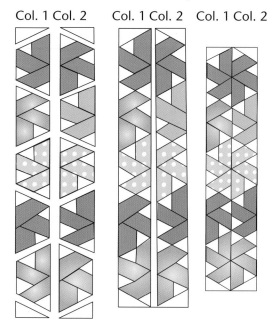

Step 4: Join the columns above, matching the seams as follows:

1. Insert a pin straight through the point where the seams meet (A).

2. Keeping this pin straight, insert a pin on either side (B).

3. Remove the center pin (C). Stitch the seam, sewing exactly across the center point.

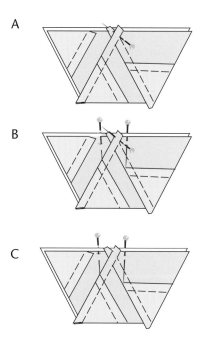

Step 5: Press column seams open.

WHIRLIGIG - 55" x 68"

Pieced by Sarah Campbell, Harrisburg, PA
Quilted by Robin Malloy, Hummelstown, PA

YARDAGE - WHIRLIGIG PROJECTS	CRIB	TWIN	DBL	QUEEN	KING	LAP	WALL
Fabrics 1 - 5 A pieces (each)	3/8	1	1 3/8	1 1/2	1 3/8	1/2	1/4
Fabric 6 - B pieces	1/2	2	2 1/2	3	2 3/4	1	3/8
Fabric 6 - End pieces	1/8	1/8	1/4	1/4	1/4	1/4	1/8
Border 1	1/2	5/8	3/4	3/4	3/4	1/2	3/8
Border 2	1	1 7/8	2	2	1 1/2	1 3/8	1/2
Border 3*	0	0	0	0	2 1/2	0	0
Backing	2 1/2	6 1/2	8 1/4	8 1/4	10	3 3/4	1 3/8
Binding	1/2	3/4	7/8	1	1	5/8	1/2

* Not shown

See pages 43–44 for basic construction of the Texas Trellis block. The yardage chart is on page 45.

Fabrics:

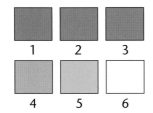

1 2 3
4 5 6

NUMBER OF PIECES NEEDED

PROJECTS	CRIB	TWIN	DBL	QUEEN	KING	LAP	WALL
Fabrics 1 - 5 (A pieces) each	34	144	180	198	188	65	24
Fabric (B pieces)	168	720	900	990	936	324	120
Fabric 6 (End pieces)	16	32	40	44	48	24	16

Number of pieces in	¹/₄ yard	¹/₂ yard	1 yard
A Pieces	30	70	140
B Pieces	66	154	300

Step 1: Join A and B pieces as shown below. Press the seams toward the A piece. Note that all B pieces are Fabric 6.

Step 2: Join the pieced triangles to form half hexagon units. Make units with each of the 5 fabrics and label each color set Unit A, Unit B, etc. Press seams toward the A piece.

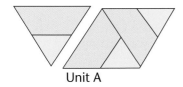

Unit A

Step 3: Join the units into columns, beginning and ending with end pieces as shown in step 2 on page 44. Let the sharper points of the end pieces extend. Press the seams in the odd numbered columns up, press the seams in the even numbered columns down.

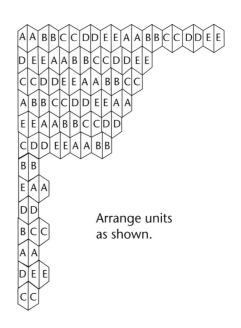

Arrange units as shown.

Step 4: Join columns matching the centers following the block assembly plan on page 48.

NUMBER OF COLUMNS AND UNITS

PROJECTS	CRIB	TWIN	DBL	QUEEN	KING	LAP	WALL
Columns across	8	16	20	22	24	12	8
Units down	7	15	15	15	13	9	5
Total units	56	240	300	330	312	108	40

Step 5: Add borders as shown on page 10.

CUT BORDER AND BINDING WIDTHS (INCHES)

PROJECTS	CRIB	TWIN	DBL	QUEEN	KING	LAP	WALL
Border 1	2	2	2	2	2	2	2
Border 2	5	6	6	6	4	6	4
Border 3	0	0	0	0	7½	0	0
Binding	2¼	2¼	2¼	2¼	2¼	2¼	2¼

Step 6: Quilt, bind, and enjoy!

47

Block Beauty ■ Donna Poster

WHIRLIGIG DESIGN AND BLOCK ASSEMBLY PLAN BY QUILT SIZE

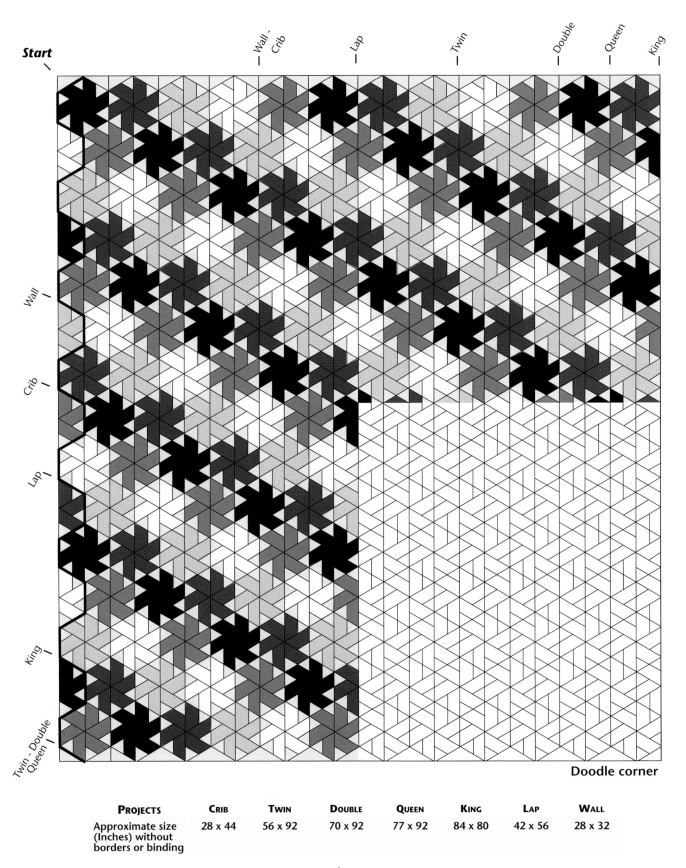

Doodle corner

PROJECTS	CRIB	TWIN	DOUBLE	QUEEN	KING	LAP	WALL
Approximate size (Inches) without borders or binding	28 x 44	56 x 92	70 x 92	77 x 92	84 x 80	42 x 56	28 x 32

TAPESTRY - 55" x 71"

Pieced by Suzanne Epler, Middletown, PA
Quilted by Laurel Cook, Mechanicsburg, PA

YARDAGE - TAPESTRY PROJECTS	CRIB	TWIN	DBL	QUEEN	KING	LAP	WALL
Fabrics 1, 2 & 3 (A pieces)	1/2	1 3/4	2 1/4	2 1/2	2 1/4	3/4	3/8
Fabrics 4, 5 & 6 (B pieces)	1/4	7/8	1	1 1/8	1	3/8	1/4
Fabric 7 (Edge pieces)	1/8	1/8	1/4	1/4	1/4	1/4	1/8
Border 1	1/2	5/8	3/4	3/4	3/4	1/2	3/8
Border 2	1	1 7/8	2	2	1 1/2	1 3/8	1/2
Border 3*	0	0	0	0	2 1/2	0	0
Backing	2 1/2	6 1/2	8 1/4	8 1/4	10	3 5/8	1 3/8
Binding	1/2	3/4	7/8	1	1	5/8	1/2

* Not shown

TAPESTRY

See pages 43–44 for basic construction of the Texas Trellis block. The yardage chart is on page 49.

Fabrics:

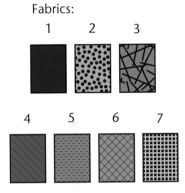

NUMBER OF PIECES NEEDED

PROJECTS	CRIB	TWIN	DBL	QUEEN	KING	LAP	WALL
Fabrics 1, 3 & 5 (A pieces) each	66	270	318	342	312	108	40
Fabrics 2, 4, & 6 (B pieces) each	56	240	300	330	312	108	40
Fabric 7 (End Pieces)	8	16	40	44	48	24	16

Step 1: Join the A & B pieces as shown. Sew fabric 1 to 2, fabric 3 to 4, and fabric 5 to 6. Press the seams toward the A piece.

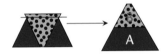

Step 2: Join the pieced triangles to form the half hexagon units. Press the seams toward the A piece.

Step 3: Join the units to form columns, beginning and ending with end pieces. Let the sharper points of the end pieces extend. Press the seams in the odd number columns up. Press the seams in the even number columns down.

Col. 1 Col. 2   Col. 3 Col. 4   Col. 5 Col. 6

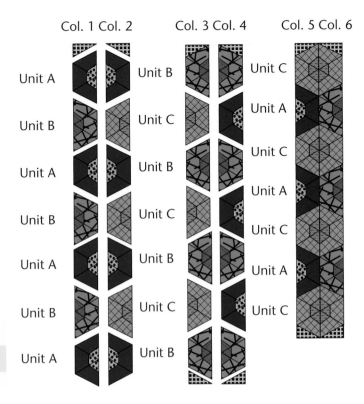

NUMBER OF COLUMNS AND UNITS

PROJECTS	CRIB	TWIN	DBL	QUEEN	KING	LAP	WALL
No. of Columns	8	16	20	22	24	12	8
Units per column	7	15	15	15	13	9	5
Total pieces	56	240	300	330	312	108	40

Step 4: Join the columns according to the layout shown below. Match the seams at the central points. Use the block assembly plan on page 52 as a guide.

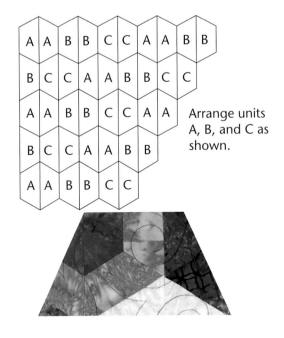

Arrange units A, B, and C as shown.

Step 5: Add borders as shown on page 10.

CUT BORDER AND BINDING WIDTHS (INCHES)

PROJECTS	CRIB	TWIN	DBL	QUEEN	KING	LAP	WALL
Border 1	2	2	2	2	2	2	2
Border 2	5	6	6	6	4	6	4
Border 3	0	0	0	0	7½	0	0
Binding	2¼	2¼	2¼	2¼	2¼	2¼	2¼

Step 6: Quilt, bind, and enjoy!

TAPESTRY DESIGN AND BLOCK ASSEMBLY PLAN BY QUILT SIZE

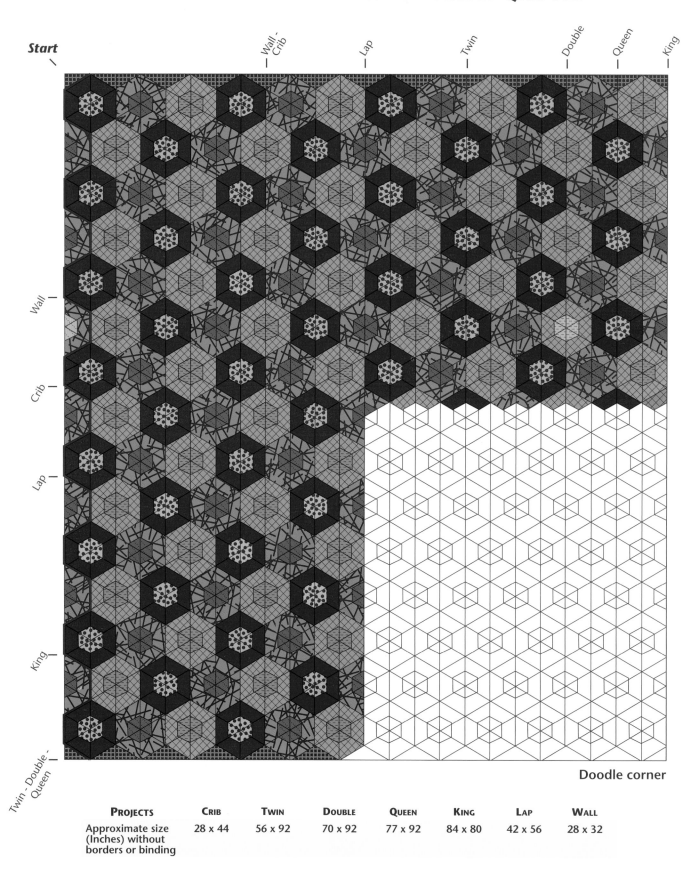

Start

Wall - Crib

Lap

Twin

Double

Queen

King

Wall

Crib

Lap

King

Twin - Double - Queen

Doodle corner

PROJECTS	CRIB	TWIN	DOUBLE	QUEEN	KING	LAP	WALL
Approximate size (Inches) without borders or binding	28 x 44	56 x 92	70 x 92	77 x 92	84 x 80	42 x 56	28 x 32

RICKRACK - 54" x 76"

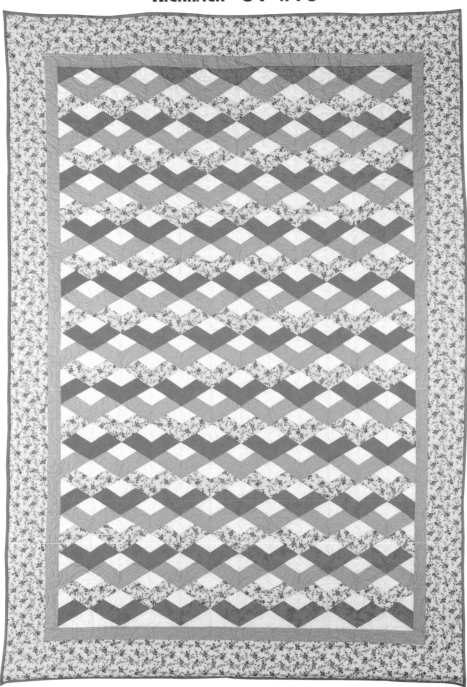

Pieced by Melinda Sheppard, Palmyra, PA
Quilted by Sherri Fleming, Hershey, PA

YARDAGE - RICKRACK PROJECTS	CRIB	TWIN	DBL	QUEEN	KING	LAP	WALL
Fabrics 1, 2, & 3 each (A pieces)	$^1/_2$	2	2	2	$2^3/_8$	$^7/_8$	$^1/_4$
Fabric 4 - Background (B pieces)	$^7/_8$	$2^1/_2$	$2^3/_8$	$2^3/_8$	3	1	$^1/_4$
End pieces fabric	$^1/_4$	$^1/_4$	$^1/_4$	$^1/_4$	$^1/_4$	$^1/_4$	$^1/_8$
Border 1	$^1/_2$	$^5/_8$	$^3/_4$	$^3/_4$	$^3/_4$	$^1/_2$	$^3/_8$
Border 2	1	$1^1/_4$	1	$1^1/_4$	$1^1/_2$	$1^1/_8$	$^1/_2$
Border 3*	0	0	$1^7/_8$	$1^7/_8$	$2^3/_8$	0	0
Backing	$2^1/_2$	$6^1/_2$	8	$8^1/_4$	10	$3^1/_2$	$1^1/_8$
Binding	$^1/_2$	$^3/_4$	$^7/_8$	1	1	$^5/_8$	$^1/_2$

* Not shown

RICKRACK

See pages 43–44 for the basic construction of the Texas Trellis block. The yardage chart is on page 53. The end piece fabric will vary according to the size of your quilt.

Fabrics:

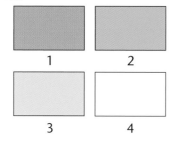

NUMBER OF PIECES NEEDED

PROJECTS	CRIB	TWIN	DBL	QUEEN	KING	LAP	WALL
Fabrics 1, 2 & 3 (A Pieces) each	64	288	280	280	336	120	24
Fabric 4 (B Pieces) Background	192	864	840	840	1,008	360	72
End Pieces Fabric	16	36	40	40	48	24	12

Step 1: Join the A and B pieces as shown below. Press seams toward the A piece.

Step 2: Join the pieced triangles to form Units 1 & 2. Press the seams of Unit 1 toward the A piece, and the seams of Unit 2 in the other direction.

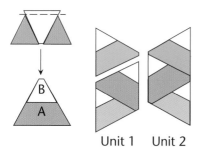

Unit 1   Unit 2

Step 3: Join the half hexagon units into columns, beginning and ending with end pieces. Let the sharper points of the end pieces extend.

Col. 1 Col. 2   Col. 3 Col. 4   Col. 5 Col. 6

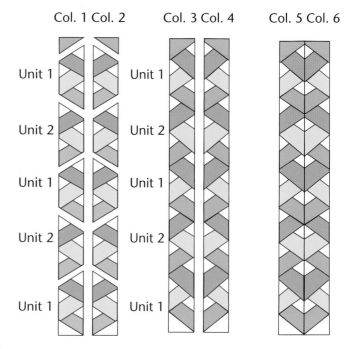

Step 4: Join the columns matching seams at the outer points of the A pieces following the block assembly plan on page 56.

COLUMNS AND UNITS PER COLUMN

PROJECTS	CRIB	TWIN	DBL	QUEEN	KING	LAP	WALL
No. of Columns	8	18	20	20	24	12	6
Units per column	8	16	14	14	14	10	4
Total units	64	288	280	280	336	120	24

Step 5: Add borders as shown on page 10.

CUT BORDER AND BINDING WIDTHS (INCHES)

PROJECTS	CRIB	TWIN	DBL	QUEEN	KING	LAP	WALL
Border 1	2	2	2	2	2	2	2
Border 2	5	4	3	3½	4	5	4
Border 3	0	0	5½	6	6½	0	0
Binding	2¼	2¼	2¼	2¼	2¼	2¼	2¼

Step 6: Quilt, bind, and enjoy!

RICKRACK DESIGN AND BLOCK ASSEMBLY PLAN BY QUILT SIZE

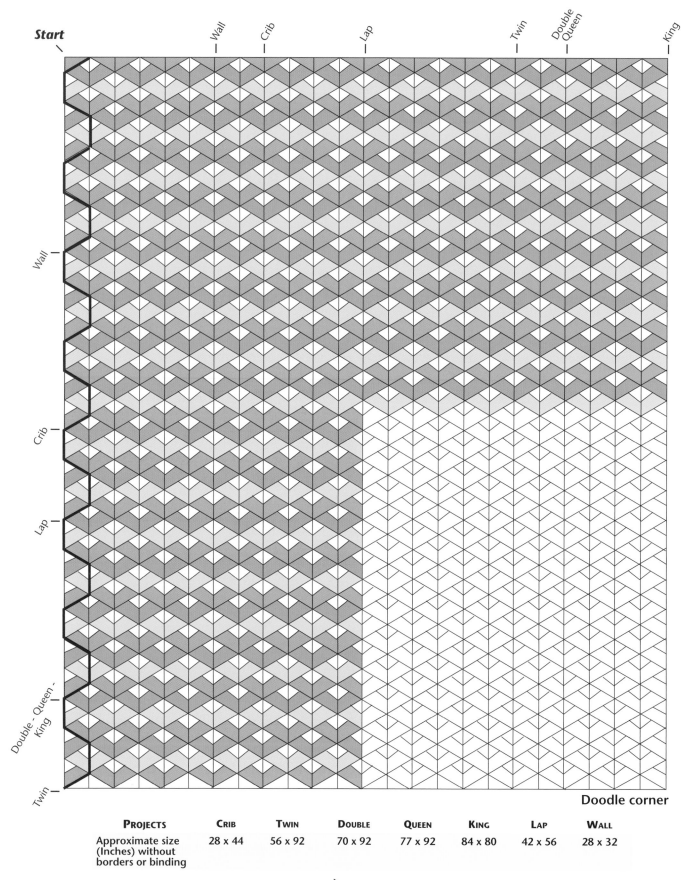

Doodle corner

PROJECTS	CRIB	TWIN	DOUBLE	QUEEN	KING	LAP	WALL
Approximate size (Inches) without borders or binding	28 x 44	56 x 92	70 x 92	77 x 92	84 x 80	42 x 56	28 x 32

CONFETTI - 58" x 70"

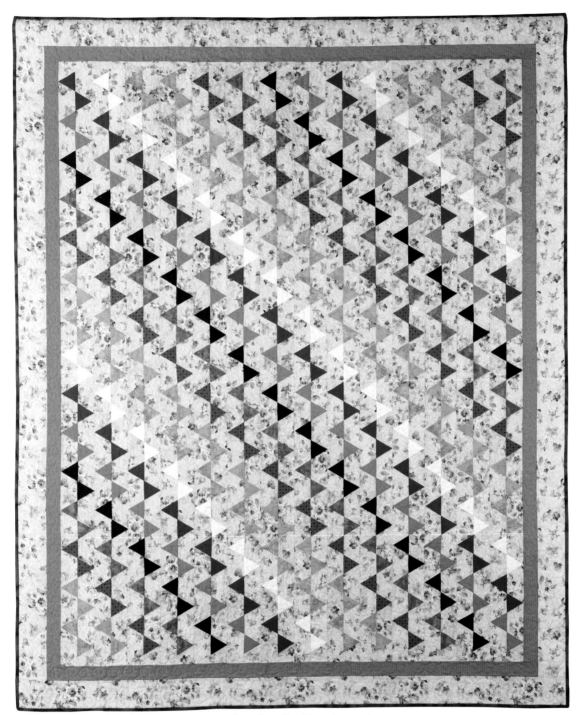

Pieced and quilted by the author
Quilted by Debbie LaDuke, Hummelstown, PA

YARDAGE - CONFETTI PROJECTS	CRIB	TWIN	DBL	QUEEN	KING	LAP	WALL
Fabric 1 - A Pieces (Background)	2¼	5½	6½	7¼	8¼	2¾	1
Fabrics 2 - 9 - B Pieces (Points) each	¼	½	½	½	⅝	¼	⅛
Border 1 (Inner)	¾	⅝	¾	¾	¾	½	⅜
Border 2 (Outer)	0	1⅜	1½	1½	2	1	⅜
Backing	3	6½	8¼	8¼	10	3¾	1¼
Binding	½	¾	⅞	1	1	⅝	½

Confetti

See pages 43 – 44 For basic construction of the Texas Trellis block. The yardage chart is on page 57.

Fabrics:

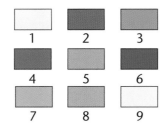

1	2	3
4	5	6
7	8	9

NUMBER OF PIECES NEEDED

PROJECTS	CRIB	TWIN	DBL	QUEEN	KING	LAP	WALL
Fabric 1 (A Pieces)	312	828	1,012	1,104	1,288	420	112
Fabrics 2 - 9 (B Pieces) each	39	104	127	138	161	53	14
Rectangles for End Pieces	12	18	22	24	28	14	8

Step 1: Join the A and B pieces as shown. Note that all A pieces are Fabric 1. Press seams toward the A piece.

Step 2: Join two matching pieced triangles to make the Basic Unit. Press the seams in either direction; isn't that nice!

Step 3: Arrange the units into columns, repeating the color sequence down the first column as shown in the block assembly plan on page 59. For the next column start dropping the units by one. Repeat this for all subsequent columns, keeping the same color sequence throughout. Join the columns beginning and ending with end pieces.

Col. 1   Col. 1   Col. 1 Col. 2

Step 4: Lay out all your columns so they form diagonal stripes. Move the left column to to the right side so it becomes the right column. Keep doing this until you like the looks of your quilt.

NUMBER OF COLUMNS AND UNITS

PROJECTS	CRIB	TWIN	DBL	QUEEN	KING	LAP	WALL
No. of columns	12	18	22	24	28	14	8
Units per column	13	23	23	23	23	15	7
Total units	156	414	506	552	644	210	56

Step 5: Join the columns, being careful not to lop off the points. To position the units, fold the A pieces in half to find the centers. Match the A center point to the points of the B pieces. Pin in place. Stitch.

Step 6: Add borders as shown on page 10.

CUT BORDER AND BINDING WIDTHS (INCHES)

PROJECTS	CRIB	TWIN	DBL	QUEEN	KING	LAP	WALL
Border 1	2	2	2	2	2	2	2
Border 2	3½	4½	4½	4½	4½	3½	2½
Binding	2¼	2¼	2¼	2¼	2¼	2¼	2¼

Step 7: Quilt, bind and enjoy!

Confetti Design and Block Assembly Plan by Quilt Size

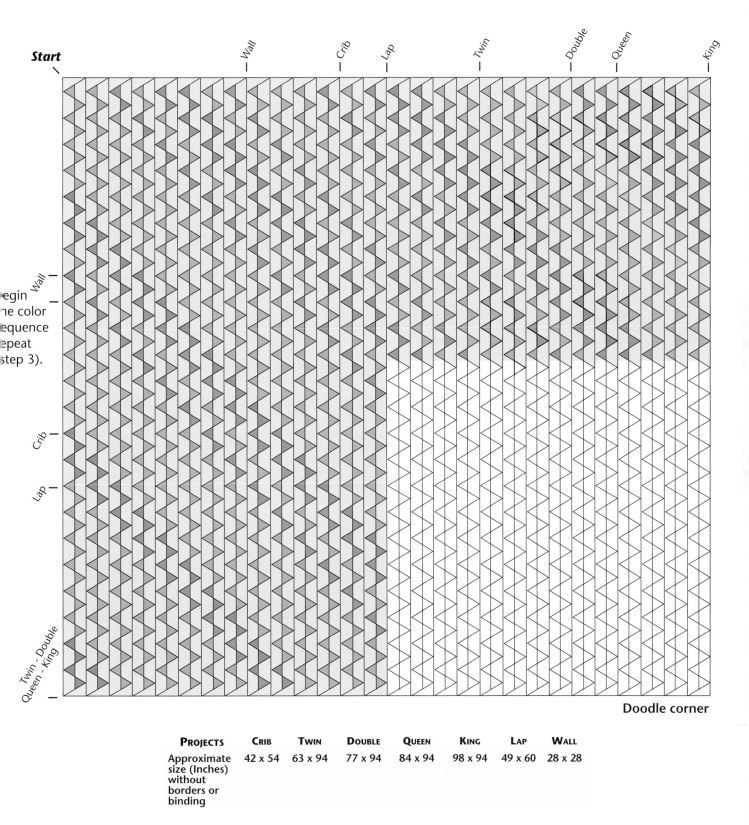

Start

Wall Crib Lap Twin Double Queen King

Begin
the color
sequence
repeat
(step 3).

Wall

Crib

Lap

Twin - Double
Queen - King

Doodle corner

Projects	Crib	Twin	Double	Queen	King	Lap	Wall
Approximate size (Inches) without borders or binding	42 x 54	63 x 94	77 x 94	84 x 94	98 x 94	49 x 60	28 x 28

Peak: Basic Construction

The 6½" Peak block is made of pairs of pieces A & D and B & C. In each block, one set of pieces A, B, C, and D will be made of the background (lighter) fabric. The other set of pieces will feature darker fabrics.

You will always sew A and D pieces together and B and C pieces together. The designs for Peak block-based quilts come from how you align the feature fabric portion of the blocks.

NIGHT AND DAY

MOUNTAINS

ZIGZAG

SPINNERS

Each quilt design in this chapter will use this block in different arrangements and will have some cutting or sewing variations, but some techniques apply to them all.

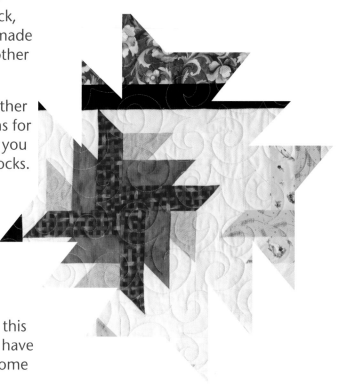

PEAK

BASIC CONSTRUCTION

Cut strips 2" wide.

From one 40" x 2" strip, you can get 6 A pieces, 8 B pieces, 11 C pieces, **OR** 20 D pieces. All designs use the same size pieces:

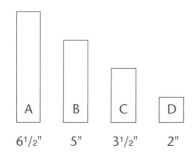

Lengths:　6¹/₂"　　5"　　3¹/₂"　　2"

Step 1: Draw seam lines on the wrong side of all the background (lightest) pieces. To do this, position the pieces **on the lines** of a gridded mat. Using a soft lead pencil or disappearing pen, mark a fine line from the upper point to 2" from the end as shown below, making a 45-degree angle.

> **HINT**: Draw *lightly across fabric,* being careful not to stretch it.

Cutting Mat

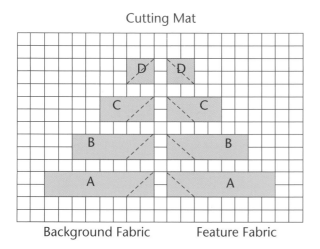

Background Fabric　　Feature Fabric

> **NOTE**: See individual patterns for seamline drawing. Some have reverse peaks and some do not.

Step 2: With right sides together, layer A and D pieces and B and C pieces. Stitch on the seam line.

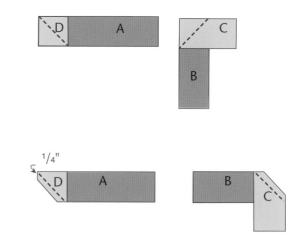

Step 3: Trim, leaving ¼" seam allowance. Unfold the pieces and press toward the darker fabric. Finished pieces should measure 6¹/₂" x 2".

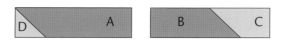

Step 4: Sew the pieced strips together to form 6¹/₂" x 6¹/₂" blocks according to the design pattern. Press seams toward the darker fabric. All seams are ¹/₄".

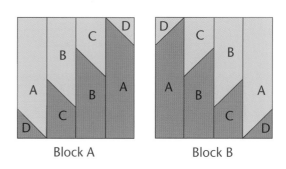

Block A　　　　　Block B

NIGHT AND DAY - 60" x 72"

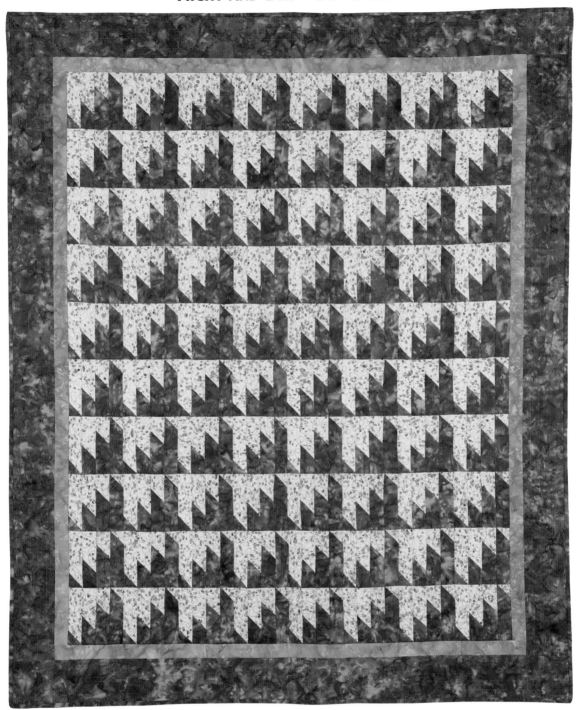

Pieced and quilted by Donna Moore, Middletown, PA

YARDAGE - NIGHT AND DAY PROJECTS	CRIB	TWIN	DBL	QUEEN	KING	LAP	WALL
Fabric 1 (Dark)	$1^1/_2$	$4^1/_2$	$5^1/_2$	$4^7/_8$	$5^5/_8$	$2^1/_2$	$^1/_2$
Fabric 2 (Light)	$1^1/_2$	$4^1/_2$	$5^1/_2$	$4^7/_8$	$5^5/_8$	$2^1/_2$	$^1/_2$
Border 1	$^1/_2$	$^5/_8$	$^5/_8$	$^5/_8$	$^3/_4$	$^1/_2$	$^3/_8$
Border 2	$^3/_4$	$1^1/_2$	$1^1/_2$	1	1	1	$^1/_2$
Border 3*	0	0	0	$1^3/_4$	$2^1/_4$	0	0
Backing	3	$6^1/_2$	8	$7^3/_4$	$9^1/_2$	$3^3/_4$	$1^1/_8$
Binding	$^1/_2$	$^3/_4$	1	1	1	$^1/_2$	$^3/_8$

* Not shown

NIGHT AND DAY

See page 60 for basic construction of the Peak block and cut piece sizes. The yardage chart is on page 62.

NUMBER OF PIECES NEEDED

PROJECTS	CRIB	TWIN	DBL	QUEEN	KING	LAP	WALL
Feature Fabrics A, B, C, D, each	48	160	192	168	196	80	16
Background Fabrics A, B, C, D, each	48	160	192	168	196	80	16

Step 1: It's important that all the 45-degree seamlines for the Night and Day design are drawn in the same direction for all fabrics.

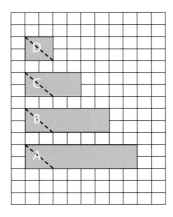

Step 2: With right sides together, layer A and D pieces and B and C pieces. Stitch on the seam line. Trim, leaving ¼" seam allowance. Unfold the pieces and press to the darker fabric. Finished strips should measure 6½" x 2".

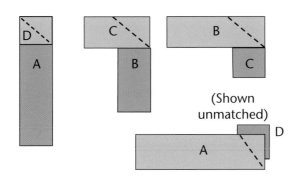

(Shown unmatched)

Step 3: Sew the strips together to form 6½" x 6½" blocks. Press seams toward the darker fabric.

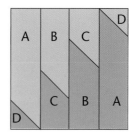

NUMBER OF BLOCKS NEEDED

PROJECTS	CRIB	TWIN	DBL	QUEEN	KING	LAP	WALL
Blocks Across	6	10	12	12	14	8	4
Blocks Down	8	16	16	14	14	10	4
Total Blocks	48	160	192	168	196	80	16

Step 4: Sew the blocks together to form rows. Press odd number rows to the right, even number rows to the left.

Fig. 4

Step 5: Sew the rows together according to the block assembly plan on page 65. Press the seams in the same direction.

Step 6: Add borders as shown on page 10.

CUT BORDER AND BINDING WIDTHS (INCHES)

PROJECTS	CRIB	TWIN	DBL	QUEEN	KING	LAP	WALL
Border 1	2	2	2	2	2	2	2
Border 2	4	5	5	3½	3½	5	4
Border 3	0	0	0	6	7	0	0
Binding	2¼	2¼	2¼	2¼	2¼	2¼	2¼

Step 7: Quilt, bind and enjoy!

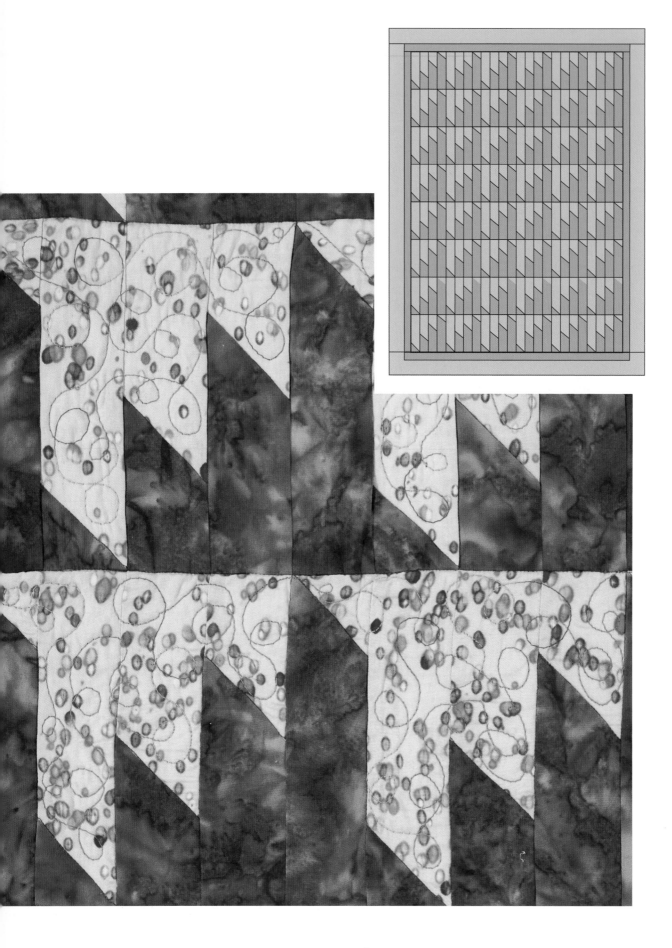

NIGHT AND DAY DESIGN AND BLOCK ASSEMBLY PLAN BY QUILT SIZE

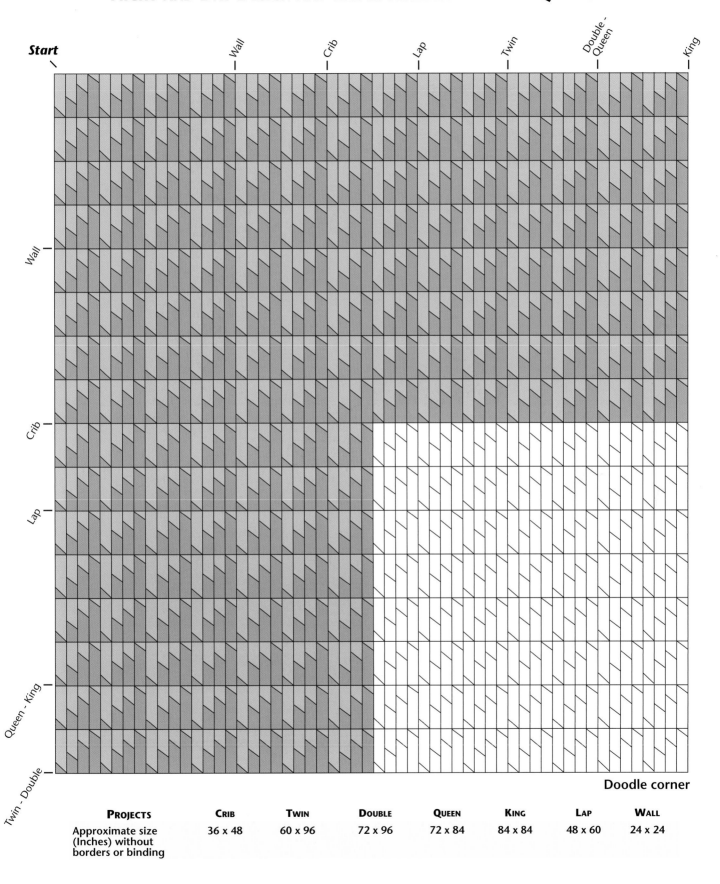

Doodle corner

PROJECTS	CRIB	TWIN	DOUBLE	QUEEN	KING	LAP	WALL
Approximate size (Inches) without borders or binding	36 x 48	60 x 96	72 x 96	72 x 84	84 x 84	48 x 60	24 x 24

Block Beauty ■ Donna Poster

Peak: Mountains

Mountains - 43" x 56"

Pieced and quilted by the author

YARDAGE - MOUNTAINS PROJECTS	CRIB	TWIN	DBL	QUEEN	KING	LAP	WALL**
Fabric 1 (Background)	$1^1/_2$	$4^1/_2$	$5^1/_2$	$4^7/_8$	$5^5/_8$	$2^1/_2$	$^1/_2$
Fabrics 2, 3, 4, 5, 6, 7 (Mountains) each	$^1/_4$	$^7/_8$	1	$^7/_8$	$1^1/_8$	$^1/_2$	$^1/_8$
Border 1	$^1/_2$	$^5/_8$	$^5/_8$	$^5/_8$	$^3/_4$	$^1/_2$	$^3/_8$
Border 2	$^3/_4$	$1^1/_2$	$1^1/_2$	1	1	1	$^1/_2$
Border 3*	0	0	0	$1^3/_4$	$2^1/_4$	0	0
Backing	3	$6^1/_2$	8	$7^3/_4$	$9^1/_2$	$3^3/_4$	$1^1/_8$
Binding	$^1/_2$	$^3/_4$	1	1	1	$^1/_2$	$^3/_8$

* Not shown ** Wall size only needs 5 Mountain fabrics

Block Beauty ■ Donna Poster

 66

MOUNTAINS

See page 60 for basic construction of the Peak block and cut piece sizes. The yardage chart is on page 66.

NUMBER OF PIECES NEEDED

PROJECTS	CRIB	TWIN	DBL	QUEEN	KING	LAP	WALL
Fabric 1, each A, B, C, D Background	48	160	192	168	196	80	16
Fabrics 2, 3, 4, 5, 6 & 7 for Mountains	8	27	32	28	33	14	4

Step 1: Draw 45-degree seamlines on the background pieces, half in one direction and half reversed as shown in step 1 on page 61.

Step 2: With right sides together, layer A and D pieces and B and C pieces. Stitch on the seam line. Trim, leaving ¼" seam allowance. Press the seams to the darker fabric. Finished pieces should measure 6½" x 2".

Block A

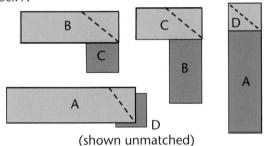

(shown unmatched)

Block B

Step 3: Sew the strips together to form 6½" x 6½" blocks. Press the seams toward the darker fabric.

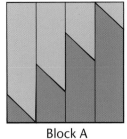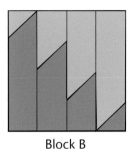

Block A   Block B

NUMBER OF BLOCKS NEEDED

PROJECTS	CRIB	TWIN	DBL	QUEEN	KING	LAP	WALL
Blocks Across	6	10	12	12	14	8	4
Blocks Down	8	16	16	14	14	10	4
Total Blocks	48	160	192	168	196	80	16

Step 4: Sew the blocks together into the rows according to the block assembly plan on page 68. Press odd number rows to the right, even number rows to the left.

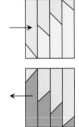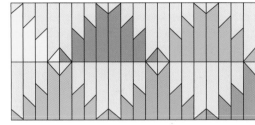

Step 5: Add borders.

CUT BORDER AND BINDING WIDTHS (INCHES)

PROJECTS	CRIB	TWIN	DBL	QUEEN	KING	LAP	WALL
Border 1	2	2	2	2	2	2	2
Border 2	4	5	5	3½	3½	5	4
Border 3	0	0	0	6	7	0	0
Binding Bias	2¼	2¼	2¼	2¼	2¼	2¼	2¼

Step 6: Quilt, bind and enjoy!

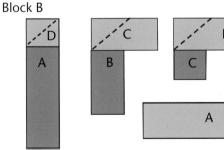

Peak: Mountains

MOUNTAINS DESIGN AND BLOCK ASSEMBLY PLAN BY QUILT SIZE

Doodle corner

PROJECTS	CRIB	TWIN	DOUBLE	QUEEN	KING	LAP	WALL
Size (Inches) without borders or binding	36 x 48	60 x 96	72 x 96	72 x 84	84 x 84	48 x 60	24 x 24

ZigZag - 46" x 58"

Pieced and quilted by the author

YARDAGE - ZIGZAG PROJECTS	CRIB	TWIN	DBL	QUEEN	KING	LAP	WALL
Fabric 1 - (Dark)	$1^1/_2$	$4^1/_2$	$5^1/_2$	$4^7/_8$	$5^5/_8$	$2^1/_2$	$^1/_2$
Fabric 2 - (Light)	$1^1/_2$	$4^1/_2$	$5^1/_2$	$4^7/_8$	$5^5/_8$	$2^1/_2$	$^1/_2$
Border 1	$^1/_2$	$^5/_8$	$^5/_8$	$^5/_8$	$^3/_4$	$^1/_2$	$^3/_8$
Border 2	$^3/_4$	$1^1/_2$	$1^1/_2$	1	1	1	$^1/_2$
Border 3*	0	0	0	$1^3/_4$	$2^1/_4$	0	0
Backing	3	$6^1/_2$	8	$7^3/_4$	$9^1/_2$	$3^3/_4$	$1^1/_8$
Binding	$^1/_2$	$^3/_4$	1	1	1	$^1/_2$	$^3/_8$

* Not shown

ZIGZAG

See page 60 for basic construction of the Peak block and cut piece sizes. The yardage chart is on page 69.

NUMBER OF PIECES NEEDED

PROJECTS	CRIB	TWIN	DBL	QUEEN	KING	LAP	WALL
Light Fabrics - A, B, C, D each	48	160	192	168	196	80	16
Dark Fabrics - A, B, C, D each	48	160	192	168	196	80	16

Step 1: Draw 45-degree seamlines on the background pieces, half in one direction and half reversed as shown in step 1 on page 61.

Step 2: With right sides together, layer A and D pieces and B and C pieces. Stitch on the seam line. Trim, leaving ¼" seam allowance. Press the seams to the darker fabric. Finished pieces should measure 6½" x 2".

Block A

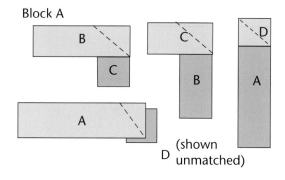

D (shown unmatched)

Block B

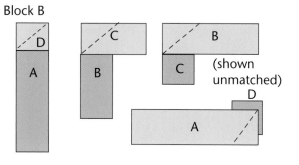

(shown unmatched)

Step 3: Sew strips together to form 6½" x 6½" blocks. Press the seams to the darker fabric. Sew the blocks together. Press odd number rows right, even number left.

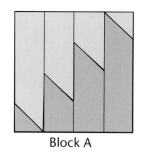
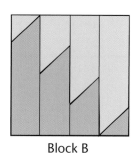

Block A   Block B

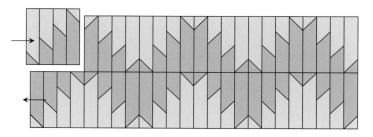

Step 4: Sew the rows together according to the block assembly plan on page 72. Press the rows in one direction.

NUMBER OF BLOCKS NEEDED

PROJECTS	CRIB	TWIN	DBL	QUEEN	KING	LAP	WALL
No. of Blocks							
Blocks Across	6	10	12	12	14	8	4
Blocks Down	8	16	16	14	14	10	4
Total Blocks	48	160	192	168	196	80	16

Step 5: Add borders as shown on page 10.

Step 6: Quilt, bind, and enjoy!

Cut Border and Binding Widths (Inches)

Projects	Crib	Twin	Dble	Queen	King	Lap	Wall
Border 1	2	2	2	2	2	2	2
Border 2	4	5	5	$3^1/_2$	$3^1/_2$	5	4
Border 3	0	0	0	6	7	0	0
Binding Bias cutting	$2^1/_4$	$2^1/_4$	$2^1/_4$	$2^1/_4$	$2^1/_4$	$2^1/_4$	$2^1/_4$

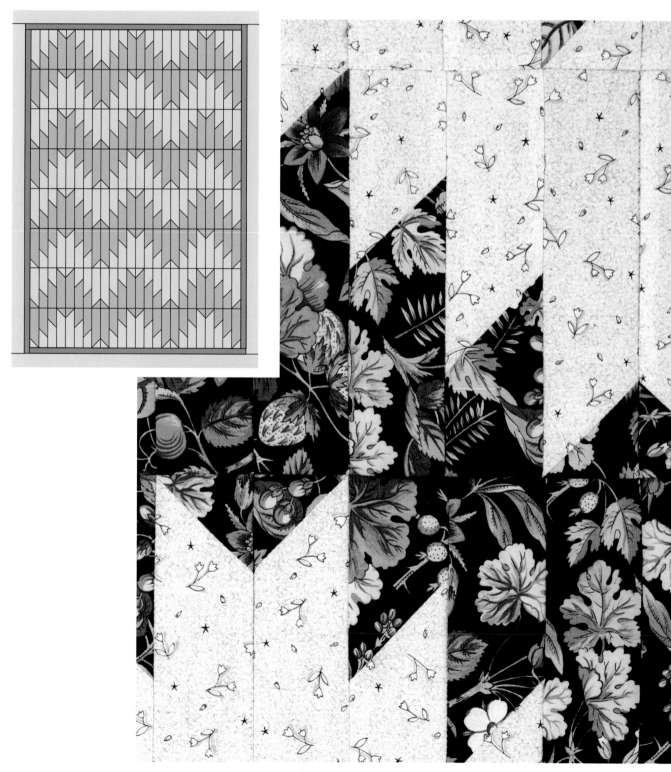

ZIGZAG DESIGN AND BLOCK ASSEMBLY PLAN BY QUILT SIZE

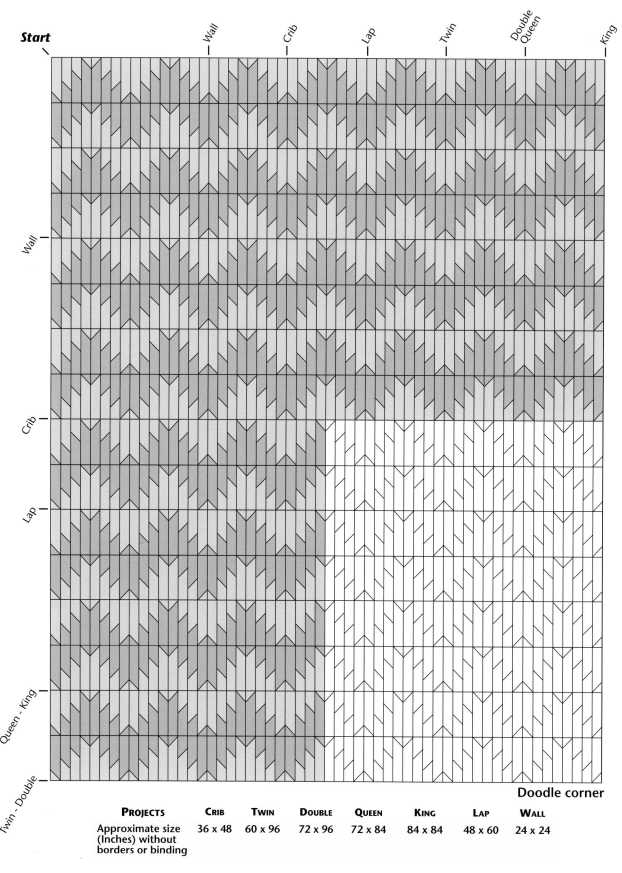

Doodle corner

PROJECTS	CRIB	TWIN	DOUBLE	QUEEN	KING	LAP	WALL
Approximate size (Inches) without borders or binding	36 x 48	60 x 96	72 x 96	72 x 84	84 x 84	48 x 60	24 x 24

SPINNERS - 58" X 70"

Pieced by Brenda Rogers, Hershey, PA
Quilted by Debbie LaDuke, Hummelstown, PA

YARDAGE - SPINNERS PROJECTS	CRIB	TWIN	DBL	QUEEN	KING	LAP	WALL
Background Fabric	1^1/$_2$	4^1/$_2$	5^1/$_2$	4^7/$_8$	5^5/$_8$	2^1/$_2$	^{1}/$_2$
Spinner Fabrics: A Pieces (Dark) 4 colors each	^{1}/$_8$	^{1}/$_2$	^{1}/$_2$	^{1}/$_2$	^{5}/$_8$	^{1}/$_4$	^{1}/$_8$
B Pieces (Medium) 4 colors each	^{1}/$_8$	^{3}/$_8$	^{3}/$_8$	^{3}/$_8$	^{3}/$_8$	^{1}/$_4$	^{1}/$_8$
C Pieces (Light) 4 colors each	^{1}/$_8$	^{1}/$_4$	^{3}/$_8$	^{3}/$_8$	^{3}/$_8$	^{1}/$_8$	^{1}/$_8$
Border 1	^{1}/$_2$	^{5}/$_8$	^{5}/$_8$	^{5}/$_8$	^{3}/$_4$	^{1}/$_2$	^{3}/$_8$
Border 2	^{3}/$_4$	1^1/$_2$	1^1/$_2$	1	1	1	^{1}/$_2$
Border 3*	0	0	0	1^3/$_4$	2^1/$_4$	0	0
Backing	3	6^1/$_2$	8	7^3/$_4$	9^1/$_2$	3^3/$_4$	1^1/$_8$
Binding	^{1}/$_2$	^{3}/$_4$	1	1	1	^{1}/$_2$	^{3}/$_8$

* Not shown

Peak: Spinners

SPINNERS

See page 60 for basic construction of the Peak block and cut piece sizes. The yardage chart is on page 73.

> **NOTE**: The "A" piece of background fabric is not pieced.

NUMBER OF PIECES NEEDED

PROJECTS	CRIB	TWIN	DBL	QUEEN	KING	LAP	WALL
Background Fabrics A, B, C, D each	48	160	192	168	196	80	16
Dark Fabric A piece	12	40	48	42	49	20	4
Medium Fabric B piece	12	40	48	42	49	20	4
Light Fabric C piece	12	40	48	42	49	20	4

Step 1: Draw 45-degree seamlines on the background pieces except for piece A. It's important that all seamlines are drawn in the same direction.

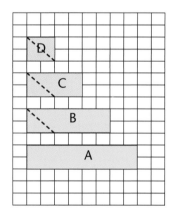

Step 2: With right sides together, layer A and D pieces and B and C pieces. Stitch on the seam line. Trim, leaving ¼" seam allowance. Press the seams to the darker fabric. Finished pieces should measure 6½" x 2".

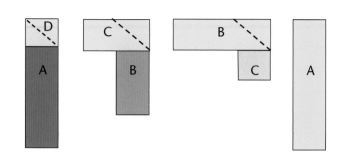

Step 3: Sew strips together to form 6½" x 6½" blocks. Press the seams to the darkest fabric.

NUMBER OF BLOCKS NEEDED

PROJECTS	CRIB	TWIN	DBL	QUEEN	KING	LAP	WALL
No. of Blocks							
Blocks Across	6	10	12	12	14	8	4
Blocks Down	8	16	16	14	14	10	4
Total Blocks	48	160	192	168	196	80	16

Step 4: Sew 4 blocks together to form a "Spinner" unit. Press all seams to the darkest strip.

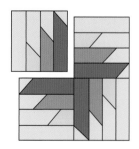

Step 5: Sew the Spinner units together to form rows. Press odd number rows to the right, even number to the left. Sew the rows together according to the block assembly plan on page 76. Press all the seams in one direction.

Step 6: Add borders as shown on page 10.

CUT BORDER AND BINDING WIDTHS (INCHES)							
PROJECTS	CRIB	TWIN	DBL	QUEEN	KING	LAP	WALL
Border 1	2	2	2	2	2	2	2
Border 2	4	5	5	3½	3½	5	4
Border 3	0	0	0	6	7	0	0
Binding	2¼	2¼	2¼	2¼	2¼	2¼	2¼

Step 7: Quilt, bind, and enjoy!

SPINNERS DESIGN AND BLOCK ASSEMBLY PLAN BY QUILT SIZE

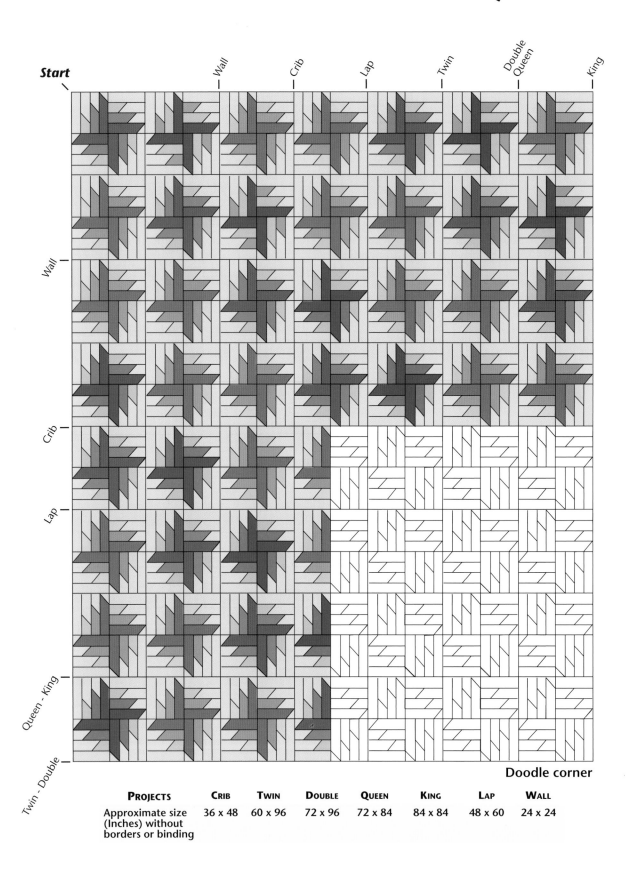

Start | Wall | Crib | Lap | Twin | Double Queen | King

Wall

Crib

Lap

Queen - King

Twin - Double

Doodle corner

PROJECTS	CRIB	TWIN	DOUBLE	QUEEN	KING	LAP	WALL
Approximate size (Inches) without borders or binding	36 x 48	60 x 96	72 x 96	72 x 84	84 x 84	48 x 60	24 x 24

Drunkard's Path : Basic Construction

The 4" Drunkard's Path block is made of templates A and B on page 78. Good contrast between the fabrics for A and B is crucial to making this block work in any design. You may trace the templates or use rotary-cutting techniques.

TRAILING VINE

LOVE RINGS

FLOWER GARDEN

FANS

Each quilt design in this chapter will use this block in different arrangements and will have some cutting or sewing variations, but some techniques apply to them all.

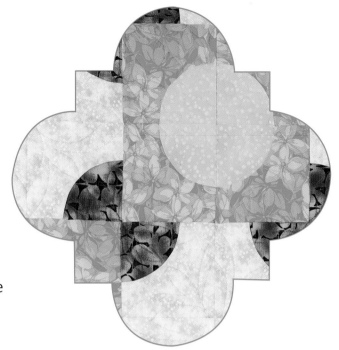

HINT: You don't need to clip these curves; the puckers will work out in the quilting. Also, allow the seams to fall where they want to. Only gently finger press the seams.

Drunkard's Path: Template Page

TEMPLATE PAGE

Step 1: *Template technique*: Cut pieces A and B.

You may create a template for A and B and cut each piece individually.

Rotary-cutting technique:

Piece A: Cut 4½" squares. You will get 8 A pieces from a 4½" x 40" strip.

Piece B: Cut 3½" x 5" rectangles. You will get 16 B pieces from a 3½" x 40" strip.

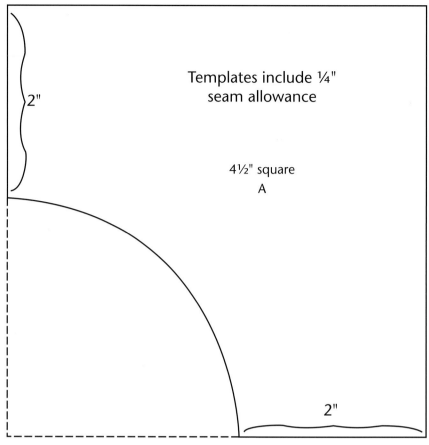

Templates include ¼" seam allowance

2"

4½" square
A

2"

Templates include ¼" seam allowance

3"

B

3"

Step 2: Cut one 5" and one 6" diameter circle from template plastic or cardboard. Carefully mark a dot in the exact center of each circle. Place the dot of the 5" circle on the lower right corner as shown. to get 1 A piece. Place the dot of the 6" circle on the upper left corner of the 3½" x 5" rectangle. Cut the curve. Repeat at the lower right corner to get 2 B pieces.

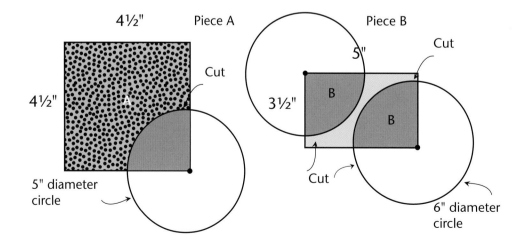

BASIC CONSTRUCTION

Step 1: Fold an A piece to find the center of the curve and pinch it to make a registration mark. In the same way mark the center of a B piece curve. Wrong sides together, match the centers and pin (A). With A on top, match the edges with your fingers and begin sewing a ¼" seam (B). When you reach the pin, remove it and match the end corners with your fingers. Press the seam to the A piece (C).

Step 2: Sew the pieced squares into units as shown. Sew the units together in the desired design. The one shown is the Trailing Vines pattern.

> **HINT**: There is no need to clip these curves as the "puckery" look will be taken up in the quilting.

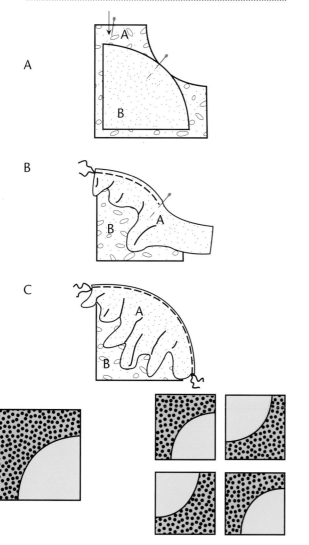

Trailing Vines

Block Beauty ■ Donna Poster

TRAILING VINES - 61" x 73"

Pieced by the author
Quilted by Debbie LaDuke, Hummelstown, PA

YARDAGE - TRAILING VINES PROJECTS	CRIB	TWIN	DBL	QUEEN	KING	LAP	WALL
Background Fabric - (A Pieces)	2	$5^1/_2$	$6^1/_8$	7	8	$3^1/_2$	1
Vine Fabric - (B Pieces)	1	$2^1/_4$	$2^1/_2$	3	$3^1/_4$	$1^1/_2$	$1/_2$
Border 1	$1/_2$	$5/_8$	$3/_4$	$3/_4$	$3/_4$	$1/_2$	$3/_8$
Border 2	$3/_4$	$1^7/_8$	2	2	$1^1/_4$	$7/_8$	$1/_2$
Border 3*	0	0	0	0	2	0	0
Backing	3	$6^1/_4$	8	8	10	4	$1^3/_8$
Binding	$1/_2$	$3/_4$	$7/_8$	1	1	$5/_8$	$1/_2$

* Not shown

TRAILING VINES

See page 78 for templates and cutting instructions and page 79 for basic construction of the Drunkard's Path block. The yardage chart is on page 80.

Fabrics:

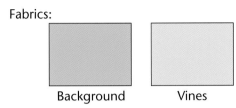

Background   Vines

NUMBER OF PIECES NEEDED

PROJECTS	CRIB	TWIN	DBL	QUEEN	KING	LAP	WALL
Background Fabric (A Pieces)	108	330	374	418	484	192	56
Vine Fabric (B Pieces)	108	330	374	418	484	192	56

Step 1: Sew A and B shapes together to make the blocks as shown. Take the page 77 hint on pressing seams in each block.

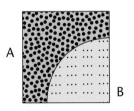

A

B

NUMBER OF BLOCKS NEEDED

PROJECTS	CRIB	TWIN	DBL	QUEEN	KING	LAP	WALL
Blocks Across	9	15	17	19	22	12	7
Blocks Down	12	22	22	22	22	16	8
Total Blocks	108	330	374	418	484	192	56

Step 2: Sew 4 blocks together to make a unit. Press the seams from half of the units to the right and up and the other half to the left and down. Alternate these units when sewing together.

Unit

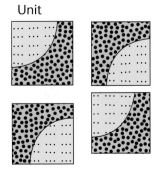

NUMBER OF UNITS NEEDED

PROJECTS	CRIB	TWIN	DBL	QUEEN	KING	LAP	WALL
No. of Units	24	77	88	99	110	48	12

Step 3: Sew the units into rows as shown on page 79. Press seams in alternating directions.

Step 4: Sew the rows together to form the design according to the block assembly plan on page 82. Press the seams in one direction.

Step 5: Add borders as shown on page 10.

CUT BORDER AND BINDING WIDTHS (INCHES)

PROJECTS	CRIB	TWIN	DBL	QUEEN	KING	LAP	WALL
Border 1	2	2	2	2	2	2	2
Border 2	4	6	6	6	$3\frac{1}{4}$	4	4
Border 3	0	0	0	0	$5\frac{1}{2}$	0	0
Binding	$2\frac{1}{4}$	$2\frac{1}{4}$	$2\frac{1}{4}$	$2\frac{1}{4}$	$2\frac{1}{4}$	$2\frac{1}{4}$	$2\frac{1}{4}$

Step 6: Quilt, bind, and enjoy.

Note: There may be blocks left over. Use them to customize the size of your quilt to add rows or columns.

TRAILING VINES DESIGN AND BLOCK ASSEMBLY PLAN BY QUILT SIZE

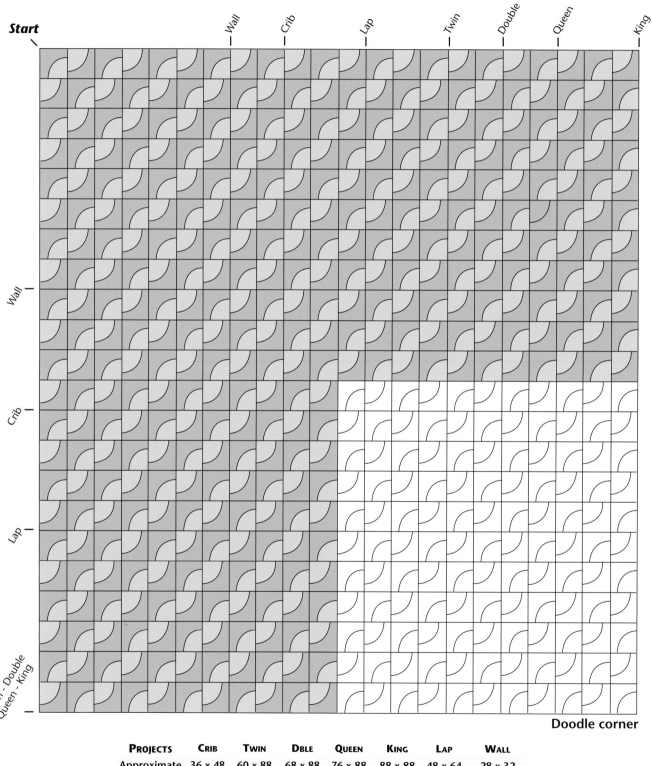

Doodle corner

PROJECTS	CRIB	TWIN	DBLE	QUEEN	KING	LAP	WALL
Approximate Size (Inches) without borders or binding	36 x 48	60 x 88	68 x 88	76 x 88	88 x 88	48 x 64	28 x 32

LOVE RINGS - 60" x 72"

Pieced by JoEllen Myers, Hershey, PA
Quilted by Emily Royle, Callaway, MD

YARDAGE - LOVE RINGS PROJECTS	CRIB	TWIN	DBL	QUEEN	KING	LAP	WALL
Fabrics 1, 2 and 3 (Rings) each	$\frac{1}{2}$	$1\frac{1}{2}$	$1\frac{3}{4}$	$1\frac{3}{4}$	2	$\frac{7}{8}$	$\frac{1}{2}$**
Fabric 4 - Background	1	$3\frac{1}{2}$	5	$4\frac{5}{8}$	$5\frac{1}{2}$	$2\frac{3}{8}$	$\frac{1}{2}$
Border 1	$\frac{1}{2}$	$\frac{5}{8}$	$\frac{3}{4}$	$\frac{3}{4}$	$\frac{3}{4}$	$\frac{1}{2}$	$\frac{3}{8}$
Border 2	$\frac{3}{4}$	$1\frac{7}{8}$	$1\frac{5}{8}$	1	$1\frac{1}{8}$	$1\frac{1}{8}$	$\frac{1}{2}$
Border 3*	0	0	0	$1\frac{7}{8}$	2	0	0
Backing	$2\frac{5}{8}$	$6\frac{1}{4}$	$8\frac{1}{2}$	$8\frac{1}{2}$	10	4	$1\frac{1}{8}$
Binding	$\frac{1}{2}$	$\frac{3}{4}$	$\frac{7}{8}$	1	1	$\frac{5}{8}$	$\frac{1}{2}$

* Not shown ** Fabrics 1 and 3 are $\frac{1}{4}$ yard each

Block Beauty ■ Donna Poster

LOVE RINGS

See page 78 for templates and cutting instructions and page 79 for basic construction of the Drunkard's Path block. The yardage chart is on page 83.

Fabrics:

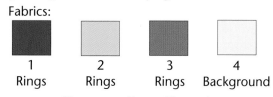

1	2	3	4
Rings	Rings	Rings	Background

NUMBER OF PIECES NEEDED*

PROJECTS	CRIB	TWIN	DBL	QUEEN	KING	LAP	WALL
Ring Fabrics 1, 2 and 3 - A and B Pieces each	16	52	72	68	84	32	4, 8, 12
Background Fabric 4 - A and B Pieces each	48	156	216	200	244	96	20

* Some sizes of the Love Rings design will not need all of these pieces, but it is easier to make extra so you can play with the layout.

Step 1: Sew shapes A and B together to form the blocks. There are six different blocks as shown. Just sew a background piece (fabric 4) to each "ring" piece and you will have it!

Fig. 1.

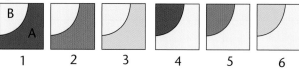

1	2	3	4	5	6

NUMBER OF BLOCKS NEEDED*

PROJECTS	CRIB	TWIN	DBL	QUEEN	KING	LAP	WALL
Blocks needed each 1 thru 6	16	52	72	68	84	32	4 to 12
Blocks Across	8	14	18	18	22	12	6
Blocks Down	12	22	24	22	22	16	6
Blocks Blocks	96	308	432	396	484	192	36

* Use remaining blocks to add to the sides and bottom as needed to complete the project.

Step 2: Join blocks into A and B units of 9 blocks each. Press Unit A seams left and down. Press Unit B seams right and up.

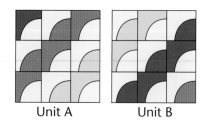

Unit A	Unit B

NUMBER OF UNITS NEEDED

PROJECTS	CRIB	TWIN	DBL	QUEEN	KING	LAP	WALL
A Units	4	12	24	20	20	8	4
B Units	4	12	24	16	16	8	0

Step 3: Sew 2 each units of A and B together, starting at the center of the quilt. Press seams of adjoining sections in opposite directions.

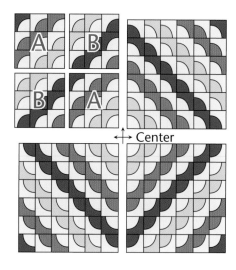

←→ Center

Step 4: Add borders as shown on page 10.

Step 5: Lay out your blocks according to the LOVE RINGS block assembly plan below or your own color arrangement.

Step 6: Quilt, bind, and enjoy!

CUT BORDER AND BINDING WIDTHS (INCHES)

PROJECTS	CRIB	TWIN	DBL	QUEEN	KING	LAP	WALL
Border 1	2	2	2	2	2	2	2
Border 2	4	6	5	3	3	5	4
Border 3	0	0	0	5$\frac{1}{2}$	5$\frac{1}{2}$	0	0
Binding	2$\frac{1}{4}$	2$\frac{1}{4}$	2$\frac{1}{4}$	2$\frac{1}{4}$	2$\frac{1}{4}$	2$\frac{1}{4}$	2$\frac{1}{4}$

LOVE RINGS DESIGN AND BLOCK ASSEMBLY PLAN BY QUILT SIZE

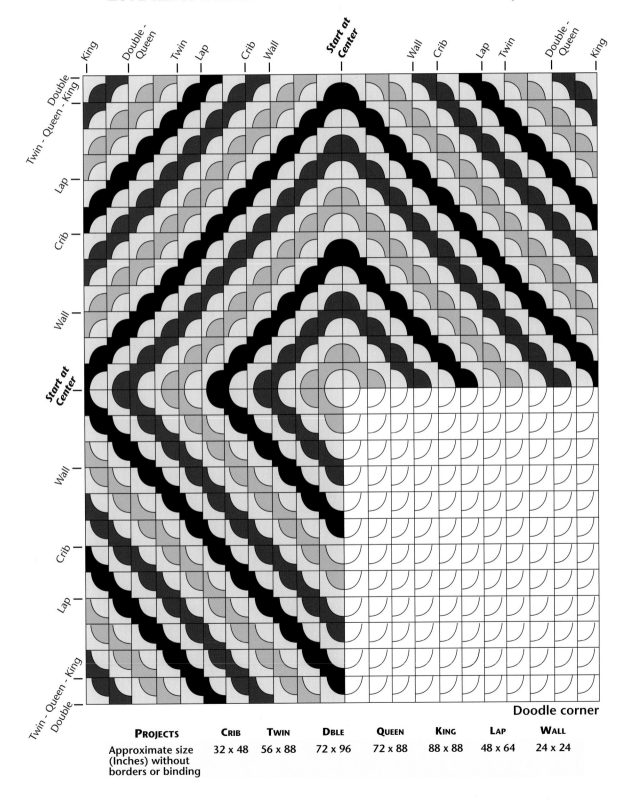

Doodle corner

PROJECTS	CRIB	TWIN	DBLE	QUEEN	KING	LAP	WALL
Approximate size (Inches) without borders or binding	32 x 48	56 x 88	72 x 96	72 x 88	88 x 88	48 x 64	24 x 24

FLOWER GARDEN - 62" x 78"

Pieced and quilted by Debbie LaDuke, Hummelstown, PA

YARDAGE - FLOWER GARDEN PROJECTS	CRIB	TWIN	DBL	QUEEN	KING	LAP	WALL
Fabric 1 - A Pieces (Flowers)	$7/8$	$3^1/4$	4	4	$4^3/4$	$1^5/8$	$5/8$
Fabric 2 - B Pieces (Flower Centers)	$3/8$	$1^1/4$	$2^1/4$	$2^1/4$	$2^3/4$	$3/4$	$1/4$
Fabric 3 - B Pieces (Leaves)	$3/8$	$1^1/4$	$2^1/4$	$2^1/4$	$2^3/4$	$3/4$	$1/4$
Fabric 4 - A Pieces (Background)	$7/8$	$3^1/4$	4	4	$4^3/4$	$1^5/8$	$5/8$
Border	$1/2$	$5/8$	$3/4$	$3/4$	$3/4$	$1/2$	$3/8$
Border 2	$1^3/4$	$3^1/4$	0	$3^1/4$	$3^1/4$	$2^1/4$	$1^1/4$
Backing	$2^1/2$	$6^1/2$	8	$8^1/2$	$9^1/2$	$3^5/8$	$1^3/8$
Binding	$1/2$	$3/4$	$7/8$	1	1	$5/8$	$1/2$

FLOWER GARDEN

See page 78 for templates and cutting instructions and page 79 for basic construction of the Drunkard's Path block. The yardage chart is on page 86.

NUMBER OF PIECES

PROJECTS	CRIB	TWIN	DBL	QUEEN	KING	LAP	WALL
Fabric 1 (A Pieces)	48	192	240	240	288	96	32
Fabric 2 (B Pieces)	48	192	240	240	288	96	32
Fabric 3 (B Pieces)	48	192	240	240	288	96	32
Fabric 4 (A Pieces)	48	192	240	240	288	96	32

Fabrics:

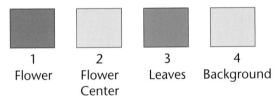

1	2	3	4
Flower	Flower Center	Leaves	Background

Step 1: Sew A and B pieces together to form the basic blocks as shown. Make half the blocks with fabrics 1 and 2, half with fabrics 3 and 4. Press seams toward the A piece.

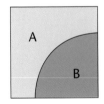

NUMBER OF BLOCKS

PROJECTS	CRIB	TWIN	DBL	QUEEN	KING	LAP	WALL
Blocks across	8	16	20	20	24	12	8
Blocks down	12	24	24	24	24	16	8
Total blocks	96	384	480	480	576	192	64

Step 2: Sew 4 blocks together to make a unit as shown. Press the seams of half of the units to the right and up and the other half to the left and down.

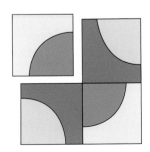

NUMBER OF UNITS

PROJECTS	CRIB	TWIN	DBL	QUEEN	KING	LAP	WALL
No. of Units	24	96	120	120	144	48	16

Step 3: Lay out the units according to the FLOWER GARDEN starting in the center.

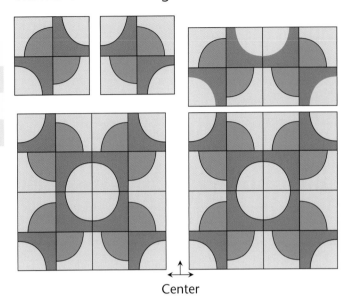

Center

Step 4: Join the units in sections, pressing the seams of adjoining sections in opposite directions. Join the sections according to the block assembly plan on page 88. Press the seams in the same direction.

> **NOTE**: Use remaining blocks to add to the sides, top and bottom as needed.

Step 5: Add borders as shown on page 10.

CUT BORDER AND BINDING WIDTHS (INCHES)

PROJECTS	CRIB	TWIN	DBL	QUEEN	KING	LAP	WALL
Border 1	2	2	2	2	2	2	2
Border 2	4	4	5	3	3	4	4
Border 3	0	0	0	4½	5½	0	0
Binding	2¼	2¼	2¼	2¼	2¼	2¼	2¼

Step 6: Quilt, bind, enjoy!

FLOWER GARDEN DESIGN AND BLOCK ASSEMBLY PLAN BY QUILT SIZE

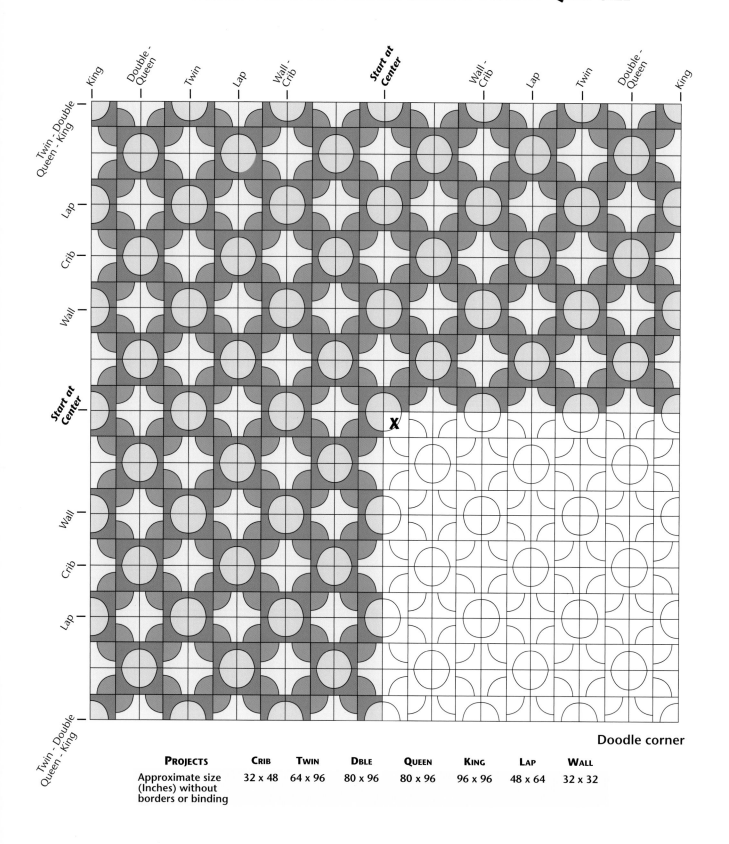

Doodle corner

PROJECTS	CRIB	TWIN	DBLE	QUEEN	KING	LAP	WALL
Approximate size (Inches) without borders or binding	32 x 48	64 x 96	80 x 96	80 x 96	96 x 96	48 x 64	32 x 32

Fans - 70" x 84"

Pieced by Joan Fischer, Hummelstown, PA, and Judie Drummond, Martinsburg, WV
Quilted by Debbie LaDuke, Hummelstown, PA

YARDAGE - FANS PROJECTS	CRIB	TWIN	DBL	QUEEN	KING	LAP	WALL
Fabric 1 - Main Motif	5/8	1 3/8	1 5/8	1 5/8	2 1/8	5/8	1/8
Fabric 2 - Center of Motif	1/2	1 1/8	1 3/8	1 3/8	1 7/8	1/2	1/4
Fabric 3 - Tassels	1/4	1/2	3/4	3/4	7/8	1/4	1/8
Fabric 4 - Border Rope	3/4	1	1 1/8	1 1/8	1 1/4	3/4	3/8
Fabric 5 - Outer Background	1	1 3/8	1 1/2	1 1/2	1 5/8	1	5/8
Fabric 6 - Inner Background	2 1/8	4 1/8	5 1/4	5 1/4	6 1/4	2 1/8	5/8
Border	0	1 1/8	1 1/4	1 7/8	2	1	3/8
Backing	3	6 1/4	8	8	10	3 5/8	1 1/8
Binding	1/2	3/4	7/8	1	1	5/8	1/2

FANS

See page 78 for templates and cutting instructions and page 79 for basic construction of the Drunkard's Path block. The yardage chart is on page 89.

Fabrics:

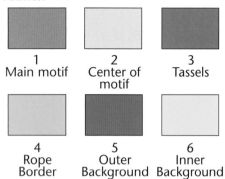

| 1
Main motif | 2
Center of
motif | 3
Tassels |
| 4
Rope
Border | 5
Outer
Background | 6
Inner
Background |

NUMBER OF PIECES NEEDED

PROJECTS	CRIB	TWIN	DBL	QUEEN	KING	LAP	WALL
Fabric 1 - B Pieces - Main Motif	72	180	240	240	300	144	12
Fabric 2 - A Pieces - Center of Motif	24	60	80	80	100	48	4
Fabric 3 - B Pieces Tassels	28	64	84	84	104	52	8
Fabric 4 - B Pieces Rope border	92	140	156	156	172	124	44
Fabric 5 - A Pieces Outer background	52	76	84	84	92	68	28
Fabric 6 - A Pieces Inner background	116	248	316	316	384	204	32

Step 1: Sew A and B pieces together to make the basic block. Press the seams toward the A piece.

BLOCKS NEEDED (INCLUDING INNER BORDER)

PROJECTS	CRIB	TWIN	DBL	QUEEN	KING	LAP	WALL
Blocks Across	12	16	20	20	24	12	8
Blocks Down	16	24	24	24	24	16	8
Blocks Blocks	192	384	480	480	576	320	64

Step 2: Sew the blocks together to form the basic, corner, and border units as shown. Finger press seams from half the blocks to the right and up and half to the left and down. Alternate these blocks when sewing them together.

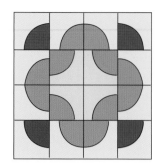

Basic unit

Corner unit   Border unit

UNITS NEEDED

PROJECTS	CRIB	TWIN	DBL	QUEEN	KING	LAP	WALL
Basic Units	6	15	20	20	25	6	1
Border Units	20	32	36	36	40	20	8
Corner Units	4	4	4	4	4	4	4

Step 3: Sew the basic units together in rows beginning and ending with border units. Construct the entire design this way. Finger press alternate rows in opposite directions.

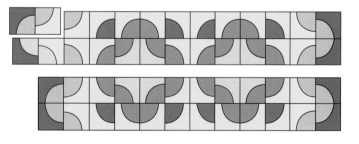

Step 4: Sew two rows of border units together including the corner units.

Step 5: Join the rows with the two border rows at the top and bottom of the design according to the block assembly plan on page 92.

CUT BORDER AND BINDING WIDTHS (INCHES)

PROJECTS	CRIB	TWIN	DBL	QUEEN	KING	LAP	WALL
Border	0	3½	3½	5½	5½	4½	2½
Binding	2¼	2¼	2¼	2¼	2¼	2¼	2¼

Step 6: Add borders as shown on page 10 (except for crib size).

Step 7: Quilt, bind, and enjoy!

FANS DESIGN AND BLOCK ASSEMBLY PLAN BY QUILT SIZE

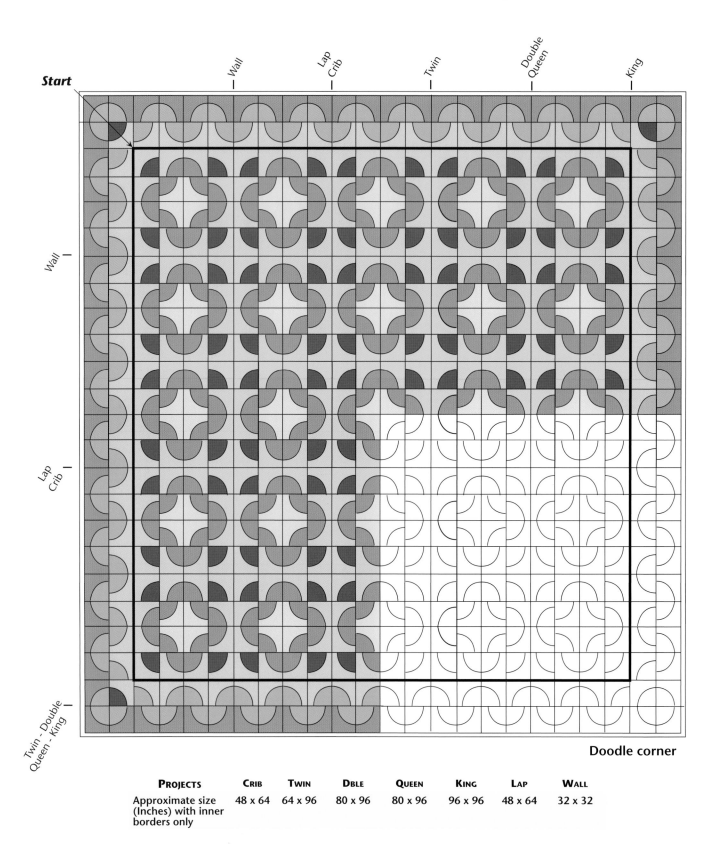

Doodle corner

PROJECTS	CRIB	TWIN	DBLE	QUEEN	KING	LAP	WALL
Approximate size (Inches) with inner borders only	48 x 64	64 x 96	80 x 96	80 x 96	96 x 96	48 x 64	32 x 32

Possible Quilting Designs

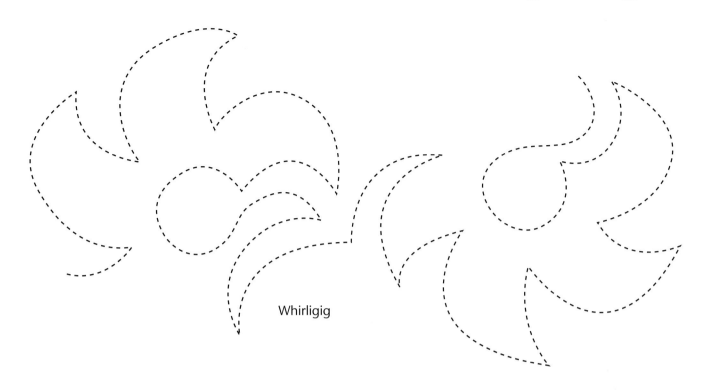

Whirligig

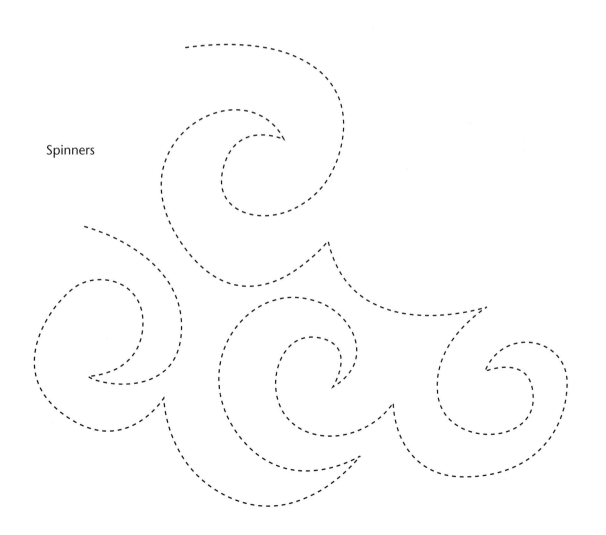

Spinners

Block Beauty ■ Donna Poster

Possible Quilting Designs

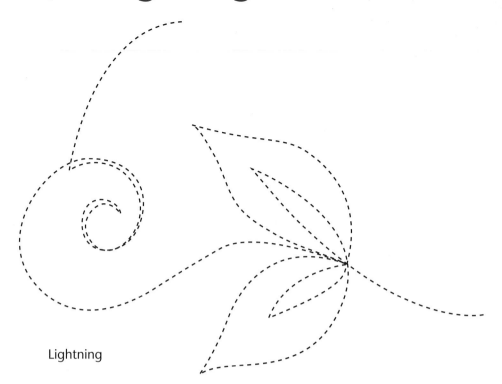

Lightning

Lattice

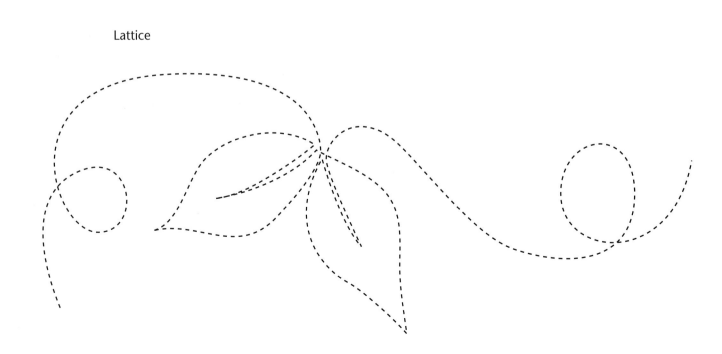

Resources

Catalogs:

Clotilde, www.clotilde.com

Batting:

Hobbs Bonded Fibers, P.O. Box 2521, Waco, TX 76710, www.Hobbsbondedfibers.com

Donna's patterns and books:

Holiday Designs, 683 Laurel Dr., Boiling Springs, PA 17007, www.quiltwithdonna.com

Educational Web site:

The Quilt Show with Ricky Tims and Alex Anderson, www.thequiltshow.com

About the Author

Why in the world do we quilters like to cut up perfectly good fabric into little pieces and then spend hours sewing it back together?

There are people who consider this close to insanity.

My own answer to this question is very clear — my mother.

Mama hated housework. She was a reluctant cook and when the mop and broom came out, my sister and I knew it was not going to be a good day.

But when Mama picked up a needle—ah, life was glorious. The sun shone brighter, the birds sang sweeter, and my mother smiled and laughed. As a toddler I loved to watch as she made a bird or flower come alive with her pretty colored stitching. I was five when I embroidered a little apron; today it hangs on the wall in my studio.

Mama and I had an agreement that I could listen to the radio if my hands were busy. By the age of eight I was making hand-worked buttonholes while Batman and Robin saved Gotham City. I darned piles of socks to the sound of clopping hooves and "Hi Yo! Silver!" It was fun and I loved the praise for my fine workmanship.

My reputation as a patient teacher comes from my mother's gentle way of showing me the finer points of stitching. I became a home economics teacher, a needlework store owner, an author of quilt books, and a lecturer.

Along the way I've taught at national quilt shows and even been on TV! And my husband, Arn, has gotten in on the act. He has invented rulers and notions for our wholesale company, Holiday Designs (www.donnaposter.com), Boiling Springs, Pa.

It is safe to say that I found in the needle a hobby, a career, and a lifetime of pleasure.

Thank you, Mama.

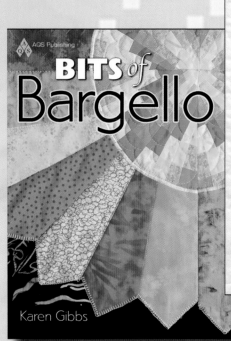

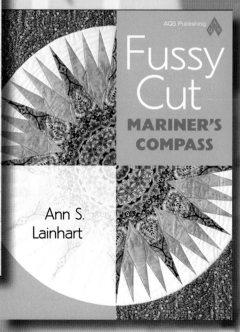